EX LIBRIS
TSM

DON'T SAY IT

By the same Author

HOW TO PRONOUNCE IT

DON'T SAY IT

ALAN S. C. ROSS

Professor of Linguistics in the
University of Birmingham

HAMISH HAMILTON

LONDON

First published in Great Britain, 1973
by Hamish Hamilton Ltd
90 Great Russell Street, London WC1
Copyright © 1973 by Alan S. C. Ross

SBN 241 02426 9

Printed in Great Britain by
Western Printing Services Ltd, Bristol

INTRODUCTION[1]

A language may be considered to consist of four parts, its pronunciation, grammar, syntax and vocabulary. The nature of the first and last of these things is obvious. The nature of the second and third of these things is not so clear. But, when we say that the genitive (or possessive) case of *cat* is, in English, formed by adding '*s* (*cat's*), that is a statement of grammar. "Syntax" has been interpreted in a variety of ways. Used loosely, the term can cover many different things—as, for instance, the use of prepositions and the articles, and word-order.

In my book *How to pronounce it*,[2] I discussed certain aspects of the pronunciation of English; in *Don't say it*, the main topic is the vocabulary. In *How to pronounce it* I tried to distinguish pronunciations as between U and non-U and as between educated and uneducated. Thus *Derby* is pronounced by the U with the first syllable to rhyme with *car*,

[1] For advice on various points I am very grateful to: Miss Joyce Ferman, Miss Frances Joly, Mrs. Larminie, Professor Lockwood and Miss Vera Lockwood, Mr. R. Machell, and to my son and daughter-in-law; and especially to my late wife. The *Sunday Times* was kind enough to publish (December 31, 1972) a request for information relevant to the present book. I received many replies to this and as a consequence of the ensuing publicity, and I am very grateful to their writers, who are unfortunately too numerous to mention.

[2] Published by Hamish Hamilton, 1970.

5

by the non-U with the first syllable to rhyme with *cur*. And the educated pronounce *amicable* with the accent on the first syllable, the uneducated with the accent on the second.

The term "U" is, essentially, an abbreviation for *Upper Class*; so "non-U" means "not of the upper class". For these terms I may refer the reader to the book *Noblesse Oblige*, edited by Nancy Mitford, in which my essay "U and non-U" appeared, to the book *What are U?*, which I edited, and to the relevant section of *How to pronounce it*.

These same two distinctions—between U and non-U and between educated and uneducated—are also valid for the vocabulary. Thus, as to the first, the non-U say *wealthy* whereas the U say *rich*. Some expressions are confined to one of the two classes; thus *receipt* meaning 'recipe' is only used by the U, and *evening meal* is only used by the non-U. Sometimes I have found it possible to characterise an expression, not only as non-U, but as lower or working class. Thus *Mister* as in *What d'you think you're up to, Mister?* is lower class, and to refer to your wife as *The Missis* is working-class. And, as to the second point mentioned above —the distinction between educated and uneducated—the expression *I bought it off of the butcher*, very frequently to be heard, is uneducated.

But, in respect of the vocabulary, there are other features to be mentioned. Some expressions are not so much non-U as definitely vulgar. As, for instance, *he gave me a raspberry*, which is as vulgar as the relevant gesture. Other expressions are merely unpleasant, though here subjectivity enters into the matter; thus I myself find the word *po-faced* unpleasant, others perhaps do not. There are also a few taboo words such as *nigger*. In the last fifty years taboo has changed; once, sexual expressions—and particularly slang sexual expressions—were taboo. This is not the case to-day; but,

6

recently, words expressing racial feeling on the part of the speaker have become taboo.

Clichés are, in the nature of the case, much used—and also, by many, much disliked. The most celebrated cliché is perhaps, still, *to leave no stone unturned*. A cliché can of course consist of a single word—a cliché-word. Thus *Relax!* must certainly be considered a cliché. And there is no reason why a cliché should not be slang, as *The rag trade* meaning 'the dressmaking business'. Words which are overworked (or overdone) are closely allied to the clichés; *pack it in* meaning 'to cease' is certainly overworked. Jargon, too, is not altogether unlike cliché; the word *project*, noun—and particularly perhaps *pilot project*—is, to most people. a jargon word. Recently the figurative use of scientific words has led to a special kind of jargon—scientific jargon. Terms of this kind are often used by people who are in ignorance of their real scientific meaning. *Osmosis*, well-known in Physics, is, for instance, much used of the interpenetration of ideas. The term *journalese* is often applied, in a derogatory fashion, to the use of clichés and jargon. This is perhaps a little unfair to journalists. Yet it is the case that their desire to write vividly —particularly in the "lower" papers—may lead them to such usages.

Some expressions are undoubtedly regarded by many people as affected. As for instance the use of *one* in reference to the speaker in *One would hardly like to do that*. Pompousness is much disapproved of to-day and there are certainly expressions regarded as pompous; for instance, *beyond a peradventure*, often used in speeches of various kinds. And there are a few expressions which I can only describe as *high-falutin*—as for instance when a stamp-collector refers to himself as a philatelist.

In talking, erudition is normally not desirable. "Here is

7

my biro pen" said the first speaker. "Ah," said the second "one of Mr. Judge's, I see." (The biro pen was invented by a Hungarian named *Bíró* and, in Hungarian, *bíró* means 'a judge'). Such remarks—very fashionable at Balliol during the twenties—are pieces of showing-off.

The question of americanisms is rather difficult. As is well-known, English to-day is full of these—as, for instance, *He is presently in Belgium*, meaning 'he is at present in Belgium'. They certainly encounter some disapproval. And, to a philologist, it does seem unfair that, while the English have borrowed many americanisms, the Americans have hardly borrowed any anglicisms, though *wangle*, an English word which became general during the First War, is used in America. But many English people like americanisms and go out of their way to employ them.

It will be inferred, then, that in *Don't say it*, I use the terms *non-U, uneducated, vulgar, unpleasant, cliché, overworked (overdone), jargon, journalese, affected, high-falutin*—and, it must be confessed, *American (americanism)*—in some sort of dis-approbation. Anything I denote as covered by one of them, is, in my own view and speech-practice, essentially a thing not to say. For the opposite concept—things which, in my own view, may legitimately be said—I use a variety of terms, such as *acceptable, correct, harmless, normal* or expressions such as *may (appropriately) be used, can be used*. I have included a very small selection of expressions, mostly slang, which may be considered harmless, as for instance, *What pestilential weather!* The reason I have done this is, in most cases, because there are some who might doubt the harmlessness of the expression and disapprobate it.

With the foregoing in mind, the method of presenting the material which I have adopted will, I think, be clear. I may note, first, that I set out interchanges as in the following

8

example:—"*A*. Will you come to lunch to-morrow?—*B*. Thanks very much", in which *A* and *B* denote the first and second speaker respectively. And, secondly, that I occasionally use the expression *inverted commas* as in the following example: "POSH. This slang word . . . is used by children of all classes. Many grown-ups use it in inverted commas." By this I mean that they indicate, by the intonation (which cannot be represented in normal printing) that they are deliberately using "a funny word".

In general, I do not consider obsolete or even obsolescent expressions, though I do mention a few. Thus I omit the non-U expression, *in Society*, and also an expression once confined to the U, *Smith of ours*, meaning 'Smith of our regiment', because enquiry among soldiers has told me that this latter has not been heard within living memory; it was once very frequent. *Pater* and *mater*, in reference to the speaker's father and mother—also *The Governor* for the former—were once U; then they were taken up by the nouveaux riches and became non-U; now the terms are dead—unless by some chance there are schools in which *pater* and *mater* survive.

Of the four linguistic domains of English mentioned at the beginning of this Introduction, there remain two, Grammar and Syntax. In the context of *Don't say it* there is virtually nothing to say about Grammar. The American *barber-shop*, instead of the English *barber's shop*, with genitival *'s*, is now very frequent. There is a curious and very old-fashioned U use in connection with the genitival *'s*, namely, not to use it in the names of shops, and to say, for instance, *I bought it at Woolworth* instead of the normal *Woolworth's*. In the verb, there is a well-known difference in the past participle of *wake*: I *was woken up, woke up*, or *waked up*. This difference has however no significance for class-distinction, or, indeed, for

9

anything else. People are simply not certain what the "correct' past participle is.

Not surprisingly, there is little to say in the field of suffixation. But there has been an increasing tendency to make new forms with *-y—crispy* instead of *crisp*. These are felt, somehow, to be more endearing, and play their part in advertising.

There are a few points which may—rather loosely perhaps —be grouped under the head of Syntax. Confusion of *I* and *me* is frequent; it is uneducated rather than non-U; for instance, *between my husband and I*. Similarly with *we* and *us* —*A better world for we conservatives*. Many people use *my* as in *my doctor, my banker, my solicitor*; this has a rather patronising effect, so other people use *the* (*the doctor, the Bank, the solicitor*). The use of *our* as in *our Ken*, meaning 'Ken, who is a member of our family', is non-U. But *my*—as in *my Richard*—is used by soppy U-mothers of their grown-up sons. To put the definite article before the names of diseases is non-U, as in *he's got the measles*. It is of course also non-U to refer to your wife as *The Wife*. So is to omit *the* before periods of time— *he worked all afternoon* instead of *all the afternoon*. The indefinite article before the names of drinks is non-U: *Will you have a coffee?* (the U say *some coffee*) or "*A*. What would you like to drink?—*B*. I'll have a whisky, please"; the U response is likely to be "Whisky, please".

There is a curious—affected, or non-U?—habit of making nouns into verbs as in *Are you teaing?*, meaning 'Are you having tea?', or, at Croquet, *Are you bisquing?*, meaning 'Are you taking a bisque?' There are three well-known uneducated verb-usages. First, the use of the past participle instead of the present participle: *He was stood there on the court, I was sat there*, instead of *He was standing* and *I was sitting*. Secondly, *I better come* instead of *I'd better come* (i.e.

I had better come). This latter is often used by the uneducated U in letters. Thirdly, *I would of come*; this arises because *'ve* in *I would've come* sounds the same as *of* in *good of you* and the speaker has confused the two things. It is rather non-U to use the auxiliary verb *do* as in *I don't have a car*, meaning '*I haven't got a car*'.

Some adverbs are formed by adding *-ly* to the adjective (*smart: He came smartly to attention*), while others are identical with the adjective (*hard: He hit the ball hard*). *Tight* in *Hold tight!* belongs to this latter class. The non-U however tend to say *Hold tightly!* (universal on buses). This is because they know vaguely that it is "correct" for an adverb to end in *-ly* and so have put the ending on in a position in which it is incorrect. It is in fact an example of something that, in respect of pronunciation, I have christened *snob-change*.[1]

The prepositions give rise to some examples. Most people say "A is different *from* B"; some say "A is different *to* B"; this latter is felt by many to be wrong and by some to be non-U; it can in fact be heard from U-speakers. There is no doubt about the third alternative, "A is different *than* B"; this is uneducated. *For* in *He had all his teeth out for free* (i.e. not paying anything) is American. In *I haven't seen him in years* the use of *in* is non-U—the U say *for*. So, too, is *of* in *Have you got change of a fiver?* (instead of U *for*). And the use of *on* both in *He's on holiday* and in "*A*. Will you have some whisky?—*B*. No thanks, I'm on beer" is also non-U. *At university*, though to-day almost invariable, especially in journalese, is undoubtedly non-U. But here it is not the preposition that is "wrong", for *at a university* or *at Oxford* is perfectly acceptable. So it is also with the non-U *he's at boarding-school*—for *at school* is acceptable. The status of

[1] I discuss this phenomenon in a note in the Czech philological journal *Časopis pro moderní filologii* (vol. 32, pages 38–39).

at table (*Do behave yourself at table!*) is something doubtful; perhaps it is old-fashioned. It is U to put *at* (underlined) before an address at which a person is staying—"A. B. Smith, Esq., *at* Claridge's". This practice is also employed when giving your own address at the head of a piece of writing-paper. The working-class frequently use *up* instead of the normal *to*—*I'm just going up the shops*. There is one jargon case of the omission of a preposition: *They agreed the proposal* (instead of *agreed to*). Somewhat similarly, *They protested the proposal*. It is not clear whether, in the somewhat similar example, *He researched the project*, a preposition has been missed out or not.

There are also cases in which a preposition is added, for instance, *Let's get it over with* and *Better face up to it*. These two last examples are not so much non-U as "bad English". Many such usages are American, such as *meet up with, come up with, stop over*—*I stopped over in Tokyo*. I am not sure of the status of to *fill out* a form, instead of *fill in*.

Wait while I come, instead of *Wait till I come* is essentially northern dialect; it is also widespread in the northern forms of standard English, such as that spoken in Leeds. Non-U— or perhaps working-class—youth have added a new conjunction to English; *like* as in *I came, like I said* (instead of *as*). And, among such people and on television, *Like the man said* has become a cliché.[1] In *It looks like we'll have a fine day, like* is uneducated for *as if*.

In matters of word-order it may be observed that *He's been very decent, has John* is non-U; and that *This I must see* (with the emphasis on *this*)—instead of *I must see this*—is a cliché.

Finally, I mention here—because there seems no other place to mention it—a curious use. Sometimes a speaker

[1] *So* instead of *so that* is well-known to be journalese and bad English —"I put in the milk first, so I can stir it in".

uses his surname (never his Christian name) in addressing himself—*Don't do that, Smith!*—as for instance if he, Smith, has made a bad stroke in a game. It is affected and annoys many people.[1]

[1] Surnames are used by the non-U as in *To do a Smith* meaning 'to behave (in some way) like Smith does'.

A: *What does A do now?* (from Bridge), meaning 'What's the next step?' Non-U.

A: *A coffee*; see p. 10.

ABJECT: *an abject apology*; see APOLOGY.

ABLE: *I asked him to come to lunch, but he was not able.* Anglo-Irish, not necessarily non-U; the English would end this sentence with *able to*.

ABOUT as in *That's what History's about.* Cliché.

ABSENCE: *Conspicuous by its absence.* Cliché.

ABSOLUTELY!, as an exclamation. Old-fashioned U, once much used by young people.

ACCENT: *Oxford accent*; see OXFORD.

ACCIDENT: *The dog's had a little accident* is essentially non-U. *Accidents will happen* and *A chapter of accidents* are clichés. *Accident-prone* is jargon, taken over from medical subjects.

ACCOMMODATION: A landlady's word for "digs".

ACCOUNT is tradesmen's talk for *bill*. *Would you like to see the account, Sir?* is a thing many U-people have blanched at.

ACTUAL: *in actual fact*; see FACT.

ACTUALLY, often pronounced *aksherly*, is a grossly overdone word, used by many people, perhaps mostly children, as little more than a mark of punctuation.

ADAM: *Adam and Eve*: see LAD.

ADAMANT, adjective—*he is adamant that . . .* Jargon.

ADORABLE, as, for instance, of a dog. This is a female use, and was certainly once U.

14

ADVERT and AD (for *advertisement*) are essentially non-U abbreviations.

AFFLUENT: *The affluent society* is a cliché much used by journalists.

AFTERNOON TEA: see TEA.

AFTERS, as in *What are we having for afters?*, meaning 'the course after the meat' (=U *pudding*). Essentially a working-class expression.

AGREE: *I couldn't agree more*, said in response to a remark, is non-U. (Sometimes *less* instead of *more*). *We'll agree to differ, then* is a cliché, often used rather rudely. *Agreed!*, meaning 'I/we agree', is a cliché. See also p. 12.

AGREEABLE: *I asked him to send me the documents: he was agreeable.* This use of the word is often thought to be "bad English"—presumably because the word is normally used in quite another sense (*a very agreeable afternoon*).

AGREEMENT: *In substantial agreement* is a cliché.

AID: *In aid of—What's Linguistics in aid of?*—is non-U.

AIR: *We're on the air* is a cliché of broadcasting (though it is difficult to see what else could be said), just as much as *Let's get airborne* is a cliché of flying. *Air Force*: see R.A.F.

AISLE is now used in respect of buildings, etc., other than churches. The use has probably come in from America, though it is the fact that it is known in north-country dialects.

ALAS as in *Alas, I can't manage it* is affected. In writing, it is essentially a cliché.

ALIVE: *The sort of day that makes one glad to be alive* is a cliché.

ALL: As a form of address, this is non-U. Thus *Good-morning, all!* on coming down to breakfast in a boarding-house. It is very familiar from Dixon's introductory *Evenin', all!* in the television programme, *Dixon of Dock Green*. The phrase *Don't we all?*, as in "*A.* I find these power-cuts very

15

worrying.—*B. Don't we all?*", is fairly recent, and used more by the non-U than by the U. *All right?*, meaning, essentially, 'Have you understood what I said?'—"*A. Eight twenty-nines are 232; all right?*"—is also non-U. *All right?* is, oddly enough, a Birmingham way of saying *Good morning!*; this has a curious effect on those who do not know the expression and have a hangover. *All that,* as in *Psychology and all that,* or *all that bunk,* is overdone. *Sorry and all that* is an annoying apology for a serious misdemeanour.

ALL-TIME: *An all-time low*; see LOW.

ALMA MATER: This expression could hardly be used to-day except as a joke.

ALONG: *I'll go along with that,* meaning, essentially, 'I agree', is a cliché, rather non-U.

ALTERNATE: In American, this is used instead of *alternative,* and this can he heard in this country too—*I've got alternate plans.*

AMPLE: *I've had ample, thanks.* Non-U. *Ample opportunity*; see OPPORTUNITY.

AMUSING: *How amusing!* is a response by elderly U women to an anecdote or the like which they have not found amusing, but boring.

ANGLE, as in *The police angle on the matter is rather different.* Jargon.

ANIMAL: It was (still is?) U occasionally to refer to a horse as an *animal. Brigadier Gerard is certainly a splendid animal. Dumb animals*; see DUMB.

ANNIVERSARY: *It's our anniversary to-day,* meaning that of our wedding, is non-U. The U say *wedding-day.*

ANON as in *I'll come anon* is facetious and rather non-U.

ANSWER: *The young know all the answers*; cliché, rather non-U.

16

ANTI as in *When it comes to pollution, he's very anti*. This seems a harmless piece of slang.

APARTMENT: *Apartments* is a landlady's expression for *rooms*.

APOLOGY: *An abject apology* is a cliché.

APPLIANCE, meaning 'a truss' or some other medical device— *my appliance*—is non-U.

APPOINTMENT: *I've got an appointment at six* is either non-U or pompous. *I've got to see someone at six* is better.

AROUND: *I'll come around six*, meaning 'about six', is an americanism, now considerably used.

ARTICLE: *It's just the article* meaning 'it's the right thing for the job' is non-U. So used to be—still is?—*article* meaning 'chamber-pot'—*D'you want to use the article?* That this last use was still current not so very long ago is shown by the following remark attributed to Churchill in answer to something said to him by the Archbishop of Canterbury. "*Archbishop.* We've got forty-eight bedrooms at Lambeth. —*Churchill.* How d'you manage, you've only got Thirty-Nine Articles?"

AS: *As of now*; see NOW.

ASCERTAIN: *I will ascertain, sir.* This used to be said by butlers and the like, and is no doubt used by their modern equivalents.

ASK: *If you ask me*, as in *If you ask me, she doesn't know what she is talking about.* Cliché.

ASPERSION: *To cast aspersions* is a cliché. It is no better in a facetious form, *Are you casting nasturtiums?*

ASPIDISTRA: The thing, rather than the word, has long been known as non-U.

ASS: *Don't be such a silly ass.* Such expressions, essentially U, continue. *The Law is an ass*; see LAW.

ASSIGNMENT, meaning a task to be done—*Your assignment is* . . . is an americanism.

ASSOCIATE: *I don't associate with people like that* is non-U.

ASSUREDLY is a pompous word.

ASTERISKED: a euphemism for *bloody* or some stronger swear-word, is no longer used, because, in most instances, the actual swear-word can be printed.

ASTROLOGY: The uneducated confuse this, a non-science, with *Astronomy* "the Queen of the sciences".

ASTRONOMICAL is used by journalists and others to mean 'very large'—*the cost will be astronomical*. This is of course because there are large numbers in Astronomy, such as the number of atoms in the universe, and many distances.

ASYLUM: *Lunatic asylum* is to-day either old-fashioned or taboo. *Mental hospital* is widely used instead.

AT: see p. 11. *At all*. The uneducated can add this to almost any sentence—*Have you seen my spanner at all?* At the end of a sentence *at all, at all* is used to denote an Irishman —*I don't like the look of the weather at all, at all*. The Irish actually do say it; it is a translation of *i n-aon ċor i n-aon ċor*.

ATOM: *To split the atom* has now become a cliché. So has *atomic* in *the atomic age*; it is used by advertisers—*Grammars for the atomic age*, promoting elementary grammars of languages.

ATTENTION: To put *Attention Mr. Smith* after the name of a firm is business jargon.

AUNTIE: In its straightforward meaning of 'aunt' (either alone, as in *Auntie says*, or with a name, *Auntie Mabel says*) this is non-U. *Auntie Times* and *Auntie BBC*—it is to-day difficult to see the justification for these expressions—are well-known affectations.

AU PAIR: To refer to an au pair girl as *The au pair* is non-U.

AU REVOIR: *Au reservoir* was a facetious alternative, essentially non-U.

AUSPICIOUS: *On this auspicious occasion* is a cliché used in speeches.

AUSSIE, often used of Australians—*He's an Aussie*. It is difficult to know whether Australians mind being called this; they can surely not object to expressions such as *Aussie dollars*.

AUTOMOBILE: This was once nouveau riche for *motor-car*. In England the term only survives in the name of the AA.

AVENUE: *To explore every avenue* is such a celebrated cliché that it may be doubted whether anyone would to-day dare to use it.

AVERAGE: *The law of averages* is highly esteemed by the General Public. Thus, if Red has turned up fourteen successive times at Roulette, then, "by the law of averages", Black is more likely to turn up than Red on the next spin —which, of course, is not the case.

AWFULLY: *Thanks awfully!*, usually pronounced *awfly*, was— and undoubtedly still is—much used by the U. The non-U use it as a standard expression when they, sarcastically, imitate the U.

AWKWARD is much used by those pretending to speak dialect, an annoying habit—*Now he's being awkward*.

AXE: *To have no axe to grind* is a cliché.

B. AND B.: see GUEST.

B—: *Not b— likely* is hardly heard to-day, as there is nothing against saying *bloody*. The old joke *Well, then, I'd better b— off* (i.e. *be off*) seems also obsolescent.

BACK, noun: *Mind your back!* meaning, really, 'Get out of the way', is working-class. *Get off my back*, meaning 'Don't be a nuisance to me', is non-U.

BACK, adverb: *Back to square one*; see SQUARE.

BACK, verb: *Back down*, meaning 'to reverse' a car, is non-U, no doubt arising with the garage-hands.

BACKSIDE: This is a very frequent word to-day, particularly, perhaps, in such expressions as *sitting on their backsides all day, doing nothing*. Many people find it unduly hearty and dislike it.

BAD meaning 'ill', as *I was bad in the night*—the expression is particularly associated with diarrhoea—is non-U. There is a curious recent use as in "*A*. So I shall be getting a thousand a year more, at least.—*B*. That can't be bad"— meaning that it's very good. *Not so bad* is a non-U response to *How d'you do?* For *Bad show*, see SHOW.

BAG: *It's in the bag* is cliché-slang, slightly non-U. *She's an awful old bag* is not a nice thing to say about a woman. *Overnight bag* is non-U, but there is no U term for the concept.

BALANCE: *On balance* is a cliché-expression.

BALLY: This was once much used by U schoolboys as a euphemism for *bloody*. It is hardly heard now.

BANDWAGON: *To jump on the bandwagon* is a cliché, of American origin, for, in England, the term *bandwagon* is without a non-figurative meaning.

BANG: *Bang on!*, meaning 'exactly right', is cliché-slang.

BANGER meaning 'sausage' and also 'motor car' (*an old banger*). Neither expression seems particularly objectionable.

BAR: *I bar that man*, meaning 'I don't like him' (often because he is non-U). This U schoolboy expression seems to have died out.

BARBER-SHOP: see p. 9.

BARGE: *I wouldn't touch it with a barge-pole* is a cliché. So also is *I don't want to barge in, but . . .* , and a rather annoying one.

BARMY as in *you're barmy!* may still be heard and seems harmless.

BASHING as in *Paki-bashing, queer-bashing*, going on an expedition to knock Pakistanis or homosexuals about. Working-class, perhaps even criminal.

BASICALLY: *Basically, of course, you're perfectly right.* Jargon.

BASINFUL: *We certainly got a basinful on that land-rover journey*, meaning 'had a rough time'. Cliché-slang.

BASTARD: Much used by all classes, and applied to things as well as people—*that spanner's a right bastard* (though this particular kind of expression is non-U). The old euphemism *basket* is still to be heard, often as a term of endearment—*Hurry up, you old basket!*

BATH: *I'm just going to take a bath* is non-U. The U for it is *I'm just going to have my bath.* The implication of the use of *my* is that the U have more baths than the non-U; this used to be true and, astonishingly, still is. There are however some very dirty U people.

BATTLE-AXE: *Look at that old battle-axe* (of a woman). Perhaps rather overdone.

BE: *Be that as it may* is a cliché.

BEAN: *Old bean!* as a form of address, or as in *He's rather a nice old bean*, is obsolescent. The use of the word as in "*A.* How much have you got in your C account?—*B.* Not a bean!" still survives.

BED: *I went on the bed* is non-U for 'I had a rest'—after lunch, as it might be.

BEDSPREAD: see COUNTERPANE.

BEG: *beg pardon*; see PARDON.

21

BEGGAR: This used to be employed as a confused euphemism
—*The poor beggar's got cancer.* Here the word intended is
really *bugger*, but *poor* goes well with *beggar*. The well-
known card-game is called *Beggar-my-neighbour* by the U
and *Strip-Jack-naked* by the non-U.

BEGINNING: *The beginning of the end;* see END.

BEHIND, noun. This was the U word for the part of the body.
It is now not much used.

BELIEVE: *Believe it or not* is a cliché. So is *Believe you me!* and
this latter is non-U. There is a curious use of the word in
Maths slang—*do you believe Equation 21?* i.e. do you believe
it to be true? *I could hardly believe my eyes;* see EYE.

BELLY-LAUGH is a cliché word.

BELT: *Belt up!* meaning 'Shut up!' was originally Royal Air
Force slang; it is now widely used.

BEND, noun: *It's enough to drive you round the bend.* A much-
used expression—harmless, or is it overdone?

BEND, verb: *Mind you don't bend it* (for instance of a car or an
aircraft), meaning 'damage it'. Harmless slang. *Bent*, as in
a bent copper 'a corrupt policeman', is a piece of criminal
slang popularised by television. *Bend over backwards*,
meaning 'make terrific efforts'—"I bent over backwards
to stop you being blackballed"—is a cliché.

BEST: *Six of the best*, as in *Six of the best coming up*, used, say,
of six packets of cigarettes, by a shopkeeper. The phrase
is non-U, except, of course, in its original, flagellant
context.

BETTER: *Are you quite better now?* The word is used by the
non-U, instead of *well*. See also p. 11. *When will you be
better?* is apparently a working-class euphemism for
"When will the baby be born?" *Better half;* see HALF.

BEVVY: *What shall we have for bevvy?*, to which the answer
might be tea or coffee. Working-class.

BICARB: This affectionate abbreviation for *bicarbonate* (of soda, i.e. NaHCO₃), still the favourite home-remedy for indigestion, etc., may even now be heard.

BIG: *big deal*; see DEAL.

BIG HEAD: As an exclamation, or in a sentence (*He's a real big head*) this expression is much used by the non-U, particularly by their children.

BILBERRY: There are four standard English words for this berry, the others being *whinberry* (often spelt *wimberry*), *whortleberry* and *blaeberry*. No question of class-distinction is involved, and the word chosen depends upon the locality, i.e. ultimately upon what the berry is called in the local dialect. *Whortleberry* is definitely southern; so, too, in the main is *wimberry* (but it is also used in Derbyshire). *Blaeberry* is Scotch and Irish and is used in the North generally—and as far south as Shropshire. *Bilberry* is widespread.

BIN meaning 'lunatic asylum', as in *He's in a private bin*. This harmless expression may still be heard.

BIND: *It's an awful bind* meaning 'bore'. This piece of Royal Air Force slang has been rather overdone. *Binding* can thus mean 'boring'. It can also mean 'causing constipation'—*Eggs are very binding*. This latter use is certainly vulgar, possibly non-U.

BIRD meaning 'girl' or 'woman'. This originally working-class expression is now almost universal, though it is often used facetiously. Elderly U people would incline to regard it as vulgar. *Bird of passage*; see PASSAGE.

BIRTHDAY: The American *Happy birthday!* is now very frequent instead of the English *Many happy returns!* The use of the American expression often involves the singing of the song *Happy birthday to you!*

BITCH: Among the U this word was once taboo—*lady-dog*

23

was used of the actual animal. But, even in those days, doggy U females were allowed to say *bitch*. Nowadays the word is considered harmless—particularly in its figurative use (*Betty really is a bitch*) and derivatives; *bitchy*; *bitchiness*; *bitch*, verb (*do stop bitching*).

BITE: *Two bites at the cherry*; see CHERRY.

BLACK, of people, is taboo when used by white people, but correct when used by black people.

BLACKLEAD, meaning 'a pencil'. Possibly, this old working-class expression no longer survives.

BLAEBERRY: see BILBERRY.

BLESS: To say *Bless you!* instead of *Thank you!* is affected, and rather non-U. *God bless!*; see GOD.

BLOKE: This slang word may still appropriately be used— *He's quite a good sort of bloke, really*.

BLOOD: *It makes one's blood boil* is a cliché.

BLOODY: This, still the most frequent expletive, is of course everywhere permitted to-day. However, even to-day, not every elderly U female likes a conversation interlarded with the word. Some people particularly dislike the use of the word as an adverb, as in *I'm going to bloody die*.

BLOW: *So I just blew*, meaning 'I left the place, I went off'. Rather affected. *Blow one's top*; see TOP.

BLOWER meaning 'telephone'—*Better get on the blower to him*. This piece of slang has been overworked.

BLUE: *A bolt from the blue* is a cliché.

BOARDING-SCHOOL: see p. 12.

BOB: *Bob's your uncle!*, meaning 'everything is all right'. Overdone, and, possibly, non-U.

BOB: *That'll cost a bob or two* is a present-day non-U replacement of an earlier, normal cliché, *That'll cost a pretty penny*.

24

BOG meaning 'lavatory'. This word has a certain currency, though it is difficult to say among which classes.

BOGGLE: *The mind boggles* is a cliché.

BOGY meaning 'policeman'. Vulgar—often to be heard on television.

BOIL: *It makes one's blood boil*; see BLOOD.

BOILER: *That old boiler!* is not a kind way of referring to a woman.

BOLSHIE: This word has almost ceased to mean 'communist', as it once used to. But it is still to be heard as in *He's being bolshie*, meaning 'he's being difficult', i.e. against authority.

BOLT: *A bolt from the blue*, see BLUE.

BONHOMOUS meaning approximately 'anxious to get on with others'. This slang word, once used by the U as well no doubt by others, is little heard to-day.

BONKERS: as in *You're bonkers!*, meaning 'You're mad' is widely used among all classes, except perhaps for the elderly U.

BONNY: This word is no doubt correctly used in Scotland. In England it is applied particularly to babies—*Isn't she bonny?*—by women, and has rather an affected sound.

BOOK is the almost universal non-U word for *magazine*. The use would seem to imply that the non-U do not read many actual books, but this may not be true. *In my book* meaning 'according to me'—*In my book twice twenty-nine is fifty-eight*—is overdone. So also is *I threw the book at him. To take a leaf out of someone's book*; see LEAF.

BOOZER, originally no doubt a working-class word for 'pub', is much used on television and, no doubt, by many people.

BOTTOM: This is to-day a very frequent word for this part of the body, used by speakers of all classes. Many people find

it vulgar. *Park your bottom* is certainly a very vulgar way of saying *Do sit down.*

BOUILLON: *In the bouillon* meaning 'in the soup', i.e. in a mess, was, apparently once used—or anyhow was thought to be used—by U young men. It is not to-day.

BOX: *We'd better box clever.* A much overdone, rather non-U use.

BOY: *Old boy* was a form of address once used by the U from man to man—particularly by soldiers. It may still be heard among the elderly. *Jobs for the boys*; see JOB. *Boys' room*; see ROOM.

BRAIN: *To suck* (or *pick*) *someone's brains* is much used and is really a most unpleasant expression. To a professor, the appearance of a vulturine individual at the door of his room whose introductory remark is *I've come to pick your brains* is very disconcerting.

BRAINY: This word is used by non-intellectuals, particularly by girls, of young men. It is not non-U.

BRASS meaning 'money'. This is popularly supposed to be a hall-mark of the north-country business man. The use is in fact widespread over all the dialects, southern ones as well. *To get down to brass tacks*; see TACK.

BRAT: This word was (still is?) used by U women of their own children. It is of course very rude to use it of somebody else's children.

BREAKDOWN: Among the general public *a nervous breakdown* is usually a euphemism for mental illness. *A breakdown* (of statistics, etc.), meaning, essentially, a detailing, is jargon.

BREAKFAST: *a cooked breakfast*; see COOKED.

BREAKTHROUGH, used mostly of new discoveries in Science and Medicine, is essentially journalese.

BREATH: *The breath of one's nostrils*; see NOSTRIL.

BREW: *Brew up*, meaning 'to make tea', was Army slang.

26

Its use by non-Service people is rather affected and very frequent.

BRICK, as in *Betty's a real brick*. This is obsolete slang; it was certainly once U.

BRIEF-CASE: The word gives an impression of non-U-ness. But is there any other word for the thing?

BRIGADE: This word is often used as in *I see you've joined the late brigade*, meaning 'you're late'. The use is essentially non-U.

BRIGHT: *Bright and early* is a cliché.

BRINY: *The Briny* meaning 'the sea' was once non-U slang; it is not used to-day.

BRITAIN, BRITISH are used by many in cases in which others would say *England, English*. The use is American and is no doubt approved of by Scotch and Welsh nationalists. But, perversely, those who use these words still say *He's an Englishman* (not the American *He's a Britisher*).

BROCHURE: This is essentially a non-U word, much used by hotel-keepers and the like.

BROLLY: This slang abbreviation was used by the U, and, to some extent, still is.

BUBBLY meaning 'champagne' was a word of the nouveaux riches. It can still be heard—among the non-U.

BUD: *To nip in the bud* is a cliché.

BUDDY: see CHUM.

BUG: *He's got a bug* (or *the bug*) was a phrase considerably used by the U—it is still to be heard. In this context the word really means 'bacterium', the phrase of course referring to the contracting of an illness. But, in fact, most of the illnesses referred to by the phrase are caused by a virus (influenza, etc.).

BULL: *It's like a red rag to a bull*. Cliché.

27

BULLY meaning 'bull-terrier' is often used by women (U or non-U) who keep these dogs.

BUM: This word, for this part of the body, has a certain currency. Many find it vulgar and unpleasing, particularly when used by young girls.

BUNDLE: *A bundle of nerves*; see NERVE.

BURNING: *A burning question*; see QUESTION.

BURP, verb—and also transitive as in *to burp a baby*. Vulgar.

BUSINESS: *A matter of business*, as in *Please tell him I've come to see him on a matter of business*, is non-U. But *business matter* is normal—*His business matters weren't going well*.

BUSY (of a telephone): This American word—for the English *engaged*—is to-day considerably used in this country—*The line is busy*.

BUTTER: *The best butter* (used of flattery) is a rather affected cliché.

BUTTY is a north-country word meaning a piece of bread-and-butter spread with something (for instance, jam). Recently, chiefly owing to television, it has become widely familiar.

BY: *By and large* is a cliché.

BYE-BYE meaning *good-bye* is non-U. It is however hard for the U not to say it in response. *Go to bye-bye* (or *go bye-byes*) meaning 'go to sleep' has had a considerable vogue, probably more among the U than the non-U.

CAB used to be employed to mean 'taxi', but this use really died out long ago. However, the word is still used by affected people, and is apparently natural to Americans, who even use *cabby* for the driver, an expression even deader among normal English people.

CAD was a favourite U word; it meant either 'villain' or 'non-U person'. It is now dead.

CAKE: *piece of cake*, as in *that job will be a piece of cake*, meaning that it is very easy. Royal Air Force slang and affected if not used by a member of it.

CALL, noun, as in *I must just pay a call*, meaning 'I must just go to the lavatory'. An old-fashioned expression, it now sounds affected or even non-U.

CALL, verb: *I'll call you*, on the telephone, though American, is much used to-day in England. There was another, U, sense of *call* meaning 'to go and see someone' (usually not earlier than three in the afternoon and not later than four) in order to make their acquaintance. On new arrivals in the neighbourhood for instance. But this U habit has very nearly died out.

CAMP, adjective: This word has surely been too much used by critics.

CAN: *Can do*; see DO.

CANDY is the American for 'sweets' and has a certain currency in this country. Confectioners are inclined to apply it to particular kinds of sweets.

CAPITAL: *That's capital!*, meaning 'very good'. An old U phrase which is probably obsolete to-day.

CARD: *picture card*; see PICTURE.

CARE: *I couldn't care less* as in "My licence was endorsed—I couldn't care less". Non-U cliché.

CAREFUL; *Careful consideration*: see CONSIDERATION.

CARRIAGE: *carriage folk*. This long obsolete working-class expression for the socially exalted has been to some exten

29

resuscitated by intellectuals—*Only carriage folk will buy that book*.

CARROUSEL: This, the American word for 'roundabout', has a considerable currency in pop songs, and some outside them.

CASUAL as in *That's pretty casual* or *he was a bit casual, wasn't he?* was (is?) used by the U to indicate bad manners.

CAT: *run like a scalded cat*; see SCALDED.

CATCH: *I didn't quite catch*, meaning 'I didn't quite hear what you said', is non-U.

CATHOLIC: This is what Catholics call themselves; others call them *Roman Catholics*.

CAUTION in *he's a caution*, or, *a regular caution*. This working-class expression is not heard to-day as often as it used to be.

CAUTIOUSLY: see HOPEFULLY.

CENTRE, verb: The old, incorrect and anti-geometrical, usages *centre round* and *centre about* (instead of the correct *centre in*) continue in full force.

CEREAL or *breakfast cereal* is non-U, though the thing itself isn't. In London, at least one club seems to have given up porridge in the summer. The U probably specify what kind they'll have—*I'll have some Weetabix, please*.

CERTAIN as in *He then made a certain gesture*. This used to be journalese for 'indecent'—presumably because in those days the newspaper wouldn't have been allowed to say what the gesture was. Similarly, *He was suffering from a certain disease*. The best-known example is perhaps *She was in a certain condition*, i.e. pregnant.

CHAFF meaning 'to tease' used to be a U word, but must now be considered obsolete.

CHALET—at a holiday camp—is non-U because holiday camps are non-U.

CHALLENGE: *It's a challenge—I like the new job, it's a challenge.* Cliché.

CHAMPERS meaning 'champagne'. This rather recent expression is "hearty" and probably non-U.

CHAP: This can still be used in expressions like *He seems a very good sort of chap* or *The chap at the Bank told me.* But in general the word, once U, is dying out, and the once very frequent *old chap!* as a form of address must be dead. *Chappie*, once used by the non-U in much the same way as *chap* (*The chappie at the Bank*), is also dying.

CHAPTER: *a chapter of accidents*; see ACCIDENT.

CHARACTER as in *I don't like that character, Smith* is rather affected.

CHARISMA: This is a word much used by journalists, and, mostly, not in the sense of the Greek original: χάρισμα means 'grace' and, especially, 'the gift of God's grace'.

CHARMING! is a cliché-interjection much used by the non-U. "*A.* So then I was sick all over the table.—*B.* Charming!" Sometimes *I'm sure* is added.

CHARWOMAN: To-day charwomen do not like to be called this; it is difficult for a U person to know what to call his; certainly not *daily*. Perhaps some periphrasis is best such as *The woman who comes in*.

CHAT: *to chat someone up* seems a harmless expression.

CHAUFFEUR: Those who can afford one are, to-day, perhaps more likely to refer to him as a *driver*.

CHAUVINISTIC: This is admittedly a "hard" word. Yet it really is extraordinary that some people are so unaware of its real meaning as to use it in the sense 'lecherous'! The use is not uncommon; it derives from the well-known Women's Lib description of men as *male chauvinist pigs*.

CHECK, noun, meaning 'bill'. The americanism is much used by waitresses.

CHECK, verb, in *to check up on*. Sentences such as *It's a difficult thing to check up on* have long been considered bad by people who feel about "correct English"—*A preposition is a bad thing to end a sentence with*, and this one ends with two.

CHEERIO!: This is essentially a non-U method of saying 'goodbye'. But to-day it is so well known that probably others use it too. At all events the polite U person can hardly refrain from saying it when it has been said to him. *Cheerybye* is more facetious non-U.

CHEERS! when drinking is non-U. What does the U person reply? To say nothing, which is normal practice between two U people, is rude. *Good Health!* is affected. Many U people say *Good luck!*

CHERRY: *to take two bites at the cherry* is a cliché, somehow rather an annoying one.

CHIFFON: *chiffon pie* is non-U because the thing itself is; it is also not very nice.

CHINK, meaning 'Chinaman'. This rather old-fashioned word is, like *wog*, essentially taboo to-day on racial grounds, though, for some reason, to disparage the Chinese is not considered as heinous as to disparage black people.

CHIP: *He has a chip on his shoulder* is a cliché.

CHOOSY is probably to be considered harmless slang.

CHOPPER is certainly harmless, and originally Fleet Air Arm slang for *helicopter*. I don't know how far it may have been replaced by *whirlybird*.

CHRIST! This interjection is greatly in vogue among all classes. Many people—not all of them Christians—dislike it.

CHRONIC as in *Isn't the weather something chronic?* This working-class use still continues and may occasionally also be heard in inverted commas.

CHUFFED: *I'm very chuffed about it,* i.e. pleased. This expression has received wide currency from its overdone use on television. The word is essentially dialect—though, in the dialects, *chuff* (without the *-ed*) appears to be the more usual form.

CHUM meaning 'friend' (particularly as between boys) is probably dead—the American word *buddy* is very often used in this sense. The word does however survive as the name of a dog-food. *Chummy*, noun, meaning 'the chap in question'—*Chummy here* 'this chap beside us'—is non-U.

CHUMP: *off his chump* seems a harmless, if old-fashioned, slang expression.

CIG meaning 'cigarette' is obsolete, or at least obsolescent. *Ciggy* is very recent; it has some currency, because, at one time, The Beatles used it.

CIRCS: *under the circs.* Cliché-slang, and rather old-fashioned.

CITIZEN: *senior citizen*; see SENIOR.

CIVIL as in *The garage-man was very civil.* This is a word used by the U and, really, denotes that the person referred to "knew his place". *To keep a civil tongue in one's head*; see TONGUE.

CLAP, verb, as in *a clapped-out old car,* or, even more unpleasantly, *I ran like the clappers* meaning *'I ran like hell'.* Many—particularly perhaps young girls—use these expressions without realising their connection with *clap,* slang for 'gonorrhoea'.

CLASS: Essentially, U schools have forms, non-U ones classes. But there is to-day some blurring of the distinction.

CLASSICAL: The uneducated tend to use this where *classic* is correct—as in *a classical situation.*

CLASSIFIED, applied to documents, information, etc. This is the American term corresponding to English *secret.* It is

33

now much used by journalists in this country in application to purely English matters.

CLASSY as in *a classy restaurant*. Non-U.

CLEAN: *All good clean fun* and *Keep the party clean!* are rather ancient clichés.

CLEARLY is used in learned writing (as in *Clearly, A is nearly equal to B*) even when the matter is not clear without some thinking on the part of the reader. A French Maths student said to me "Whenever Poincaré says *évidemment*, I know I'm in for two days' hard work".

CLEVER: *box clever*; see BOX.

CLICK meaning 'to get off(with a girl)', as in P. G. Wodehouse's *The clicking of Cuthbert*, is now dead.

CLIMATE: *Climate of opinion* is a cliché—though one of very respectable antiquity; the new *Supplement* to the *Oxford English Dictionary* first records it in 1661.

CLIQUY is used by the non-U, of tennis-clubs and the like, in a very curious manner. A cliquy club should mean 'a club in which there are many cliques or factions' but the non-U use it as a synonym for another non-U word, *exclusive*, and by it they mean that the club is not friendly to them because they are non-U.

CLOAKROOM meaning 'lavatory'—*May I go to the cloakroom?*—is non-U.

CLOSE has two non-U meanings. First, as in *the room is very close* (*U stuffy*). Secondly, as in *my brother and I were very close*.

CLUE: *I haven't a clue!* is a (rather non-U?) cliché.

COACH as in *coach-tour* used to be non-U (*char-à-banc* was the U word for the then non-U thing). But now *coach* is universal. U attempts to call it a *bus* are void for ambiguity.

COCK as in *Better watch it, cock!* is vulgar; the word has been taken up by the television.

34

COCKY, meaning essentially 'conceited'. This piece of public school slang still survives among the U, particularly apropos games.

COFFEE-TABLE BOOK, indicating a somewhat ostentatious book, illustrated, is an expression much used by journalists and, to some extent, by others.

COLLEAGUE: This is used by the non-U in a rather pompous manner by persons in quite humble situations—a postman might refer to a fellow-postman as *My colleague*. There are instances however when the word is acceptable, as, for instance, of one professor referring to another at the same university.

COLLEGE: *He is at college* meaning 'at a university' is non-U.

COLLINS or *Collins letter*, meaning 'a letter thanking someone for having had you to stay'. This long-established U expression—it derives from *Pride and Prejudice*—is no longer heard to-day, except affectedly.

COLOGNE: This, the American for *eau-de-cologne*, is now used in this country also.

COME: *Come!* as an invitation to enter is affected; it is felt by some to be a more brisk and business-like form of *Come in!* The expression *Come again!* meaning, really, 'I haven't understood you', is cliché-slang. *Cigarettes coming up!* (when you have just asked for some, say, in a bar) is a non-U cliché. *There's been a lot of coming and going* is a cliché and *I didn't know whether I was coming or going* is a non-U cliché. *Come to stay*: see STAY.

COMMENCE: It is well-known that this is "bad English" for *begin*.

COMMON was once widely used by the U to mean 'non-U' (sometimes abbreviated as *comm*—"The Joneses—very comm, my dear"). But the word can hardly be heard among the U to-day. The U also used it of horses, meaning 'ill-bred', and this use may well continue.

COMMONSENSE: Expressions containing the phrase *commonsense will prevail* are felt to be clichés by many. *Commonsense is always wrong* is a more intellectual cliché.

COMPANY: *I didn't like the company at that hotel*; this is a non-U use. *Present company excepted* is a well-known cliché, still very much in use.

COMPARTMENT: *to keep in watertight compartments*; see WATER-TIGHT.

COMPETE: *I can't compete!* is a cliché—"Cynthia had five different kinds of home-made cake for tea to-day. I can't compete!"

COMPLEX: *inferiority complex*; see INFERIORITY.

COMPOTE: In hotels, *compote of fruit* means 'tinned fruit salad', rather a non-U thing.

CON, verb, as in *I've been conned*, is an expression of the working or criminal classes. It has been popularised by television. Many people dislike it. *Con-man* is presumably acceptable, for there is no other word for it—*chevalier d'industrie*, once used in English in this sense, has long been dead.

CONCERT: *concert pianist*; see PIANIST.

CONDIMENTS, non-U for 'salt, pepper and mustard'—*Pass the condiments please* (for the non-U often have them all together in one holder).

CONFERENCE: *In conference*, as in *Mr. Smith is in conference*, meaning only that he is talking to someone. Secretary's jargon.

CONFUSED, medical jargon (apropos a mental state), now much used by non-medicals.

CONGÉ: When about to leave a neighbourhood, the U were once in the habit of calling at the houses of their

36

acquaintance and leaving cards with the corners turned down and with P.P.C. (=*pour prendre congé*) written on them. This habit has died out since the last War.

CONNECT in *Only connect!* This phrase of E. M. Forster's, in *Howard's End*, has become a cliché, but many who use it do not know what the author meant by it.

CONSENSUS: *The consensus of opinion is* . . . has been overworked.

CONSIDERATION as in *I expect he'll do it for a consideration* (i.e. money) is non-U. *Your request will receive careful consideration* is a Civil Service and business cliché.

CONSOMMÉ as in *You're properly in the consommé*, meaning 'You *are* in a mess'. A facetious alteration of *in the soup*, it was once used by U young men, or anyhow by P. G. Wodehouse when writing about them; it is now defunct.

CONSPICUOUS: *conspicuous by its absence*; see ABSENCE.

CONSTITUTIONAL meaning 'a walk'. This expression, once used by the U, is probably now dead, except among the old.

CONTACT, verb, as in *You'd better contact Mr. Smith*, was originally business jargon, and is essentially non-U.

CONTEMPORARY as in *The music I've just heard on the radio was very contemporary*, meaning 'very modern', is a non-intellectual remark. The word is similarly applied to furniture.

CONVENIENCE meaning 'lavatory' is non-U officialese—*Public Conveniences* as a sign.

COOK-BOOK is the American for *cookery book*. The term is much used in English, often in titles of books as *The Spanish Cook-book*.

COOKED: *A cooked breakfast*, denoting the inclusion of at least a boiled egg, is non-U.

COOKY, adjective, applied to the clothes of children or girls, is harmless slang.

COP, noun, meaning 'policeman'. This American word is much used, in a rather facetious manner, especially on television.

COPE, verb, as in *I can cope* or *Smith will cope*, is a female word, used more by the U than by the non-U.

CORE: *Rotten to the core* is a cliché.

COSTLY meaning 'expensive' is non-U.

COSTUME meaning 'coat-and-skirt' is female non-U.

COTTAGE. *Cottage pie* is U-er than (or perhaps just more old-fashioned than?) its synonym *shepherd's pie*.

COUCH meaning 'sofa' is non-U.

COULD: *could be* meaning 'perhaps', as in "*A*. Are you going to London?—*B*. Could be", is much overworked.

COUNT: *to stand up and be counted*, meaning to make plain on which side one stands (in a meeting or the like). Cliché.

COUNTERPANE: This word is certainly U. But there are two other words for the thing, *bedspread* and *coverlet*, whose status is somewhat doubtful. The former is perhaps old-fashioned.

COURSE: *Horses for courses*; see HORSE.

COVER: *Cover up* as in *I'll cover up for you* meaning 'I'll make excuses for you' is a cliché.

COVERLET: see COUNTERPANE.

CRACKING: *He's in cracking form* seems a harmless piece of slang.

CRAFTY as in *Oh! very crafty* said, for instance, of a stroke in a game. Cliché-word.

CREATE, intransitive verb, as in *Baby isn't half creating*, i.e. kicking up a fuss. Non-U.

CREATIVE: When applied to work this is a cliché-word, especially in matters of education. For some reason, for children to-day, daubing with paints or playing at theatricals is considered more creative than learning Latin grammar by heart like a parrot or doing Algebra.

CREDIBLE is to-day an ugly word because of its application to "the nuclear deterrent". So also *credibility*.

CRETIN: This was once much-used as a term of mild abuse— *Don't be such a cretin*. To-day it is hardly heard.

CRISPY: see p. 10.

CROCKS, as for instance in the meaning 'tea-things'—*I'll wash up the crocks*. Female non-U.

CROWN: *If you say that again I'll crown you*. Vulgar.

CRUCIFY: In figurative use this is a very popular word— *If you print that they'll crucify you*. Many people find the word very unpleasant, even if they are not Christians.

CRUET: This is non-U for 'salt, pepper and mustard' in a holder. *Pass the cruet, please*.

CRUMB: *Crust or crumb?*; see CRUST.

CRUMMY (sometimes spelt *crumby*). This American word really means 'lousy'—*crumb* means 'a louse'—and, in this country, it is used in much the same way—*Her flat is a crummy sort of place*.

CRUNCH in *When it comes to the crunch*. A much-used cliché.

CRUST in *Crust or crumb?*, used by someone cutting bread to mean 'Will you have the crusty end of the loaf or a slice from the inside?' A one-time non-U phrase, no doubt still in use.

CRYSTAL-CLEAR, as in *You've made the point crystal-clear*. A cliché, usually used in a somewhat sarcastic manner.

CUFF: *Off the cuff*, of answering questions. A cliché, used by journalists and on television, apropos interviews.

CULTIVATED, as in *They're cultivated people*. There is no exact U or intellectual counterpart to this non-U expression— *civilised* is perhaps the nearest.

CULTURE is rather a joke-word, because it has been so over-done—as in the sentence "Music is culture, but Algebra isn't". *They're cultured people* (cf. CULTIVATED) is non-U. *Culture-vulture* 'one very keen on culture' used recently to be much in vogue, but it now seems obsolescent.

CUNNING: "I think I can still get a double twenty at darts, if my hand hasn't lost its cunning." Cliché.

CUP: *How is your cup?* is a non-U way of saying *Would you like some more tea? Your cup of tea* meaning 'a thing suitable for you' has been much overdone; recently this cliché has been rammed home on ITV, in an advertisement for a particular brand of tea.

CUPPA meaning 'cup of tea'. This working-class expression has been so much used in inverted commas by both U and non-U that it has become a cliché.

CURIOUSER: *Curiouser and curiouser* is a cliché (from *Alice in Wonderland*).

CURTAIN: *It's curtains*, as in "Unless profits go up sharply, it's curtains for the Firm", i.e. the Firm is done for. Cliché.

CUSTOM: *It's an old Spanish custom*—"At this pub they always put the vodka in first, then the tomato juice; it's an old Spanish custom"—is a cliché that was once used quite a lot (frequently in films). It is not much heard to-day.

CUSTOM-BUILT and -MADE, describing things made to measure or to order, is, in large part, of American origin. In England it is often used figuratively, and is somewhat of a cliché.

CYCLE is non-U for U *bike*. The verb *to cycle* is also non-U—*I cycled from Worthing to Brighton.*

CUTLERY is essentially a non-U word. A U person, washing-up (as U people do) would say *I've just got the knives and forks* (or *the silver*) *to do.*

CZECHO-SLOVAKIAN: *Do you speak Czecho-Slovakian?* is un-educated. The country has two main languages, Czech and Slovak (about as different as are German and Dutch). *Do you speak Czech?* is thus correct—for it is Czech rather than Slovak that the foreigner would learn.

D: *D-day*, meaning the day on which decimalisation of the currency was introduced. This was, naturally, a phrase of extremely short life. An official creation, it was felt by many to be in poor taste, because of D-day in the last war.

D: *Jolly D*, i.e. *jolly decent*, a phrase from a wartime radio show, was at one time much overdone. It can be used either genuinely, or sarcastically—"*A*. I'll take the car, and you can walk.—*B*. Jolly D of you".

DAD: There seems to be little class distinction as between the words people call their fathers. *Dad, daddy, father* are normal—the latter perhaps rather old-fashioned. *Pa* is a joke, *my papa* (used *of* my father) affected. *The daddy of them all*, meaning the doyen of some subject, is a cliché.

DAILY, noun: see CHARWOMAN.

DANDRUFF: Both this word and *scurf* seem unpleasant to many people—not apparently to advertisers (who use the former word). There seems no logical reason for this feeling of unpleasantness for the trivial ailment is not an indecent one.

DARK, applied to people, meaning the colour of many inhabitants of Africa and India, is to-day really a taboo-word. (*He's a dark gentleman* was once much used by

41

Oxford landladies.) It is of course a euphemism for *black*, evidently a more taboo word; at all events I heard a non-U patience player refer to the Six of Clubs as a *dark* Six, presumably because she didn't like to use the word *black*.

DARLING as a form of address had and has various affected uses. In the nineteen-twenties it was much used between U young women. Now it is often used between non-U young men, sometimes homosexual ones, and Charlie Drake's *Hallo my darlings!* has spread beyond the confines of television.

DATE, meaning what the Austrians so amusingly call a *rendezvouserl*, although an americanism, has wide currency in this country among all classes. Derivative expressions, such as *blind date* and the verb *to date* (someone), are also much used.

DAY: This word appears in a number of clichés—*It's all in the day's work, Its days are numbered, It made my day*, and *In this day and age*. Politicians seem especially to like *At the end of the day*. For *The sort of day that makes one glad to be alive*, see ALIVE.

DEAD: Used as an intensive—*She's dead stupid*—this is non-U. *Drop dead!*; see DROP.

DEADLY: meaning 'boring' was at one time a female U expression—*My dear, he's deadly*. Now it is not much heard.

DEAL: *Big deal!* This American—and sarcastic—expression has in this country become a non-U-ism, or, at least cliché-slang. A *package deal* is a cliché, much used by journalists.

DEAR: *My dear!* was of course a U, and no doubt also a non-U, form of address to women. Now it is much used by men to men; this has rather a homosexual effect. It is also used—to both men and women—to indicate South-Western dialect—and it is in fact still used in Devonshire. *My dear man*; see MAN.

DECIMATE: The verb seems to be misunderstood; at all events *badly decimated* appeared in the *Sunday Times* recently.

DECLARE: *I declare!* or *Well I declare!*, expressing annoyance, were once well-known non-U-isms. They seem to be less frequent to-day.

DECLASSÉ: This is used by the U of a U person who has become non-U. As for instance, a U woman, who, thirty years ago, married a non-U man.

DEDICATED, used of a person, is a much overdone word.

DEFENCE: A *defence mechanism* is a piece of jargon, imported from Psychology.

DEFINITELY: This has become a cliché way of saying 'Yes'—"*A.* So you're going to London.—*B.* Oh, definitely!"

DE GAULLE: "I've got something wrong with my Charles de Gaulle", i.e. gall-bladder. Very non-U. *Gaulle* is of course here pronounced the same as *gall*, while Charles receives its English, not its French, pronunciation.

DEGUT: *To degut a book* is rather affected. It is often used of someone reading it in order to review it or just reading it quickly for any reason.

DELUSION: *A snare and a delusion*; see SNARE.

DENTURE: *Dentures* is a well-known non-U-ism against U *false teeth*. Dentists however do invariably use the word.

DESIRE: *To leave much to be desired* is a cliché.

DESSERT is often to be heard in this country in its American sense of 'the course after the meat-course', thus corresponding to U *pudding* and non-U *sweet*. This is confusing because, in English, *dessert* is correctly used to mean the last course of a meal, consisting of fruit.

43

DETERRENT: *The ultimate deterrent* is a cliché, much used by journalists—and an ugly one.

DEVIL: *Talk of the Devil!* is a cliché, used when someone about whom you have just been talking appears.

DEVOUTLY: *I devoutly hope* is a cliché.

DIABOLICAL: *Diabolical skill* is a cliché.

DIALECT: The term is misused by the uneducated. Thus they will say "I suppose Estonian is a dialect", meaning that it is not a real language, whereas it undoubtedly is. This remark naturally offends Estonians. The correct use of the word is however not very straightforward. Thus English and Norwegian are two closely-related, but different languages. If they had been, not languages of civilisation, but the languages of two groups of South American Indians, they would undoubtedly have been reckoned as two dialects of one and the same language. It all depends upon how far from civilisation you are.

DICEY: This originally Royal Air Force slang word is now overworked by the general public.

DICHOTOMY: This rather learned word has now become jargon.

DICKY: *He's got a dicky heart.* This cliché—of which the exact medical meaning is left in doubt—is old-established. So also is a similar one—*Something wrong with the old ticker.*

DICTIONARY: *To swallow the dictionary* is an expression used by the non-U and uneducated in respect of someone who uses long and learned words when talking.

DIE: *You'd have died laughing*; see LAUGH.

DIFFER: *agree to differ*; see AGREE.

DIFFERENT: see p. 11.

DIG: The fairly modern meaning of this word—'be fond of' and the like—*I do dig Beethoven*—is still mostly confined to the young. However it is used by others in inverted commas.

DIM, of persons, meaning 'undistinguished'. A harmless slang expression—*Smith is really very dim*. "The dim and distant past"; see PAST.

DINNER: This is of course non-U against U *lunch*, though U dogs do have their dinner (or *din-dins*) in the middle of the day. There is a fairly recent phrase exemplified in *I've taken out more appendixes than you've had hot dinners*. It must be non-U, because it has the above non-U use of *dinner*.

DIRTY: *I've got a dirty great overdraft*; this use of *dirty great* is cliché-slang. So also is *Mathematics is a dirty word to him*.

DISAPPEAR: *I'll just disappear for a minute*, meaning 'I'm going to the lavatory', is a female euphemism, not necessarily non-U.

DISHY: This word, meaning essentially 'attractive', is genuinely used by females of many classes, but sometimes in inverted commas.

DISINTERESTED: This is used by the uneducated to mean 'uninterested'—*I am completely disinterested in Linguistics*.

DISPENSER, for sugar, razor-blades, etc. Essentially a non-U word, introduced by the sellers of these things.

DISTANT: *the dim and distant past*; see PAST.

DISTINGUISHED: *Distinguished-looking* is perhaps a rather overdone word.

DISTRESSED meaning 'mentally disturbed'. A piece of jargon introduced from Medicine.

DIVAN, i.e. divan-bed. The thing itself used to be non-U but is perhaps no longer so.

DIVINE as in *How too divine!* Female U-slang of the nineteen-twenties, now obsolescent.

DO: The various uses to consider here are best illustrated by exemplifying sentences. "*A.* Would you like some more

45

cake?—*B*. No thanks, I've done very nicely", meaning 'I've had enough', is a non-U response. So also is the use applied in other contexts as in *Arsenal are doing very nicely, thank you*. "*A*. Shall I try some jam, then?—*B*. You do that" (*or* "You do that thing"); cliché. "*A*. Have you got two dozen six inch nails?—*B*. Can do"; cliché-slang. The indecent *You know what you can do with it* is vulgar; it is widely used on television. *Don't do anything I wouldn't do* is used by the non-U in saying good-bye. *I'll do you*, meaning 'I'll beat you up' or even 'I'll kill you', is essentially criminal slang; it is often used on television. *Not done* was once used by the U of a non-U habit; the expression was a favourite of public schoolboys; it is not much heard to-day. For sentences such as *I don't have a car*, see p. 11.

DOCTOR: There is some doubt as to the use of this as a non-medical title. Fifty years ago, Ph.D.'s at Oxford and Cambridge were invariably merely addressed as "Mr."—the degree was then one fairly recently introduced. At provincial universities they tended to be called "Dr."; this was felt by Oxford to be non-U. Nowadays it is generally felt correct to call a Ph.D. "Dr.", particularly a female one. Nevertheless, in the case of a young person, it has a pompous effect. There is no doubt at all about the degree higher than a Ph.D.; a D.Litt. must certainly be called "Dr."

DODGY, as in *It's a bit dodgy*. Cliché-slang.

DOILY: The thing and therefore the word are non-U.

DOLLAR: *That's the 64,000-dollar question*. Much overworked.

DON: Correctly, this is applied only to someone who is a Fellow of a College at Oxford or Cambridge—*He is a don at Balliol*. It is therefore incorrect to apply it, as is so often done, to a member of an academic staff at any other university, or to someone who teaches at Oxford or

46

Cambridge but is not a Fellow. Newspapers invariably call all academic staff *dons*; this is because *don* is a good short word for a headline. (In a similar manner, *Premier* is used in headlines for *Prime Minister*, because it is shorter.)

DOUGHNUT: In English Mathematics and Physics this word is used to mean 'torus'. This is American and not English. American doughnuts are indeed of this shape, but true English ones are spheres.

DRAIN: *To laugh like a drain* is cliché-slang. The use has been extended, so that one may hear *He played like a drain*, meaning 'very badly'.

DRESS-SUIT, meaning 'dinner-jacket', is non-U.

DRINK: *soft drink*; see SOFT.

DRIP, of a person—*He's an awful drip*, seems a harmless piece of slang, though possibly rather an old-fashioned one.

DRIVER; see CHAUFFEUR.

DROP: *Drop dead!* is cliché-slang, much used by children.

DUCK: *Good weather for ducks* is a cliché.

DUMB: *Dumb animals* meaning just 'animals' is a cliché phrase of the stupid, not necessarily the non-U. Oddly enough in the stupid phrase *Animals always know, don't they?* the epithet *dumb* is not prefixed.

DURANCE: *In durance vile* is a cliché.

DUTCH: *To go Dutch*, meaning to share the expenses, is a slang phrase hardly used to-day.

EACH: *Each and everyone.* Cliché.

EAR: *We'll have to play it by ear.* Cliché.

EARLY: *bright and early*; see BRIGHT.

EAT as in *Shall we eat out?* or *Have you eaten?* is probably non-U, possibly only affected.

EDGE: *To have the edge on someone.* This piece of American slang seems rather harmless.

EGG: "*A.* I've brought some chocolate.—*B.* Oh, good egg!" To-day, this expression is hardly used, except perhaps facetiously. *He's rather a good egg*, meaning 'a good sort of chap', is, possibly, no longer used at all. *Egg custard*, meaning 'real custard' and not that made from custard-powder, is of course non-U, for the U have only real custard. *Have you ever made an egg custard?* is thus not an endearing thing to be said to a U hostess who has provided custard. There was a similar, but, naturally, ephemeral, expression in the last War; *shell egg*, meaning a real egg as opposed to dried egg. *Was there egg on my face!*, meaning 'Was I put to shame!' Non-U, and rather unpleasant.

EH? This is non-U against U *What?* in response to something which the speaker has not quite heard.

EIDERDOWN; see QUILT.

ELEMENTARY: *Elementary, my dear Watson!* Cliché, from Sherlock Holmes.

ELEVENSES; see LUNCH.

ELSE: *Or else!* as in "You'd better let me have that money quick—or else!" Non-U cliché-slang.

EMPIRE-BUILDER: This word, apparently first said of Cecil Rhodes, is considerably used figuratively and in a derogatory sense. *He's an empire-builder* refers to a person who is trying to expand his dominion, say, in an office. It is jargon.

END: *at the end of one's tether*; see TETHER. *The beginning of the end*; see BEGINNING; *at the end of the day*; see DAY.

ENEMY: *To be one's own worst enemy.* Cliché.

ENORMITY: Is this word really coming into uneducated use in the sense 'enormousness'? It appeared so in *The Times* recently (*the enormity of the horse*).

ENOUGH: *Enough is enough!*, meaning, really, just 'Enough!', indicating for instance that enough has been heard of a subject. Cliché.

ENTITLE: *to be entitled to one's own opinion*; see OPINION.

ERSE: An English name for the Irish language current in the nineteenth century and still used. The Irish do not like the expression at all. *Do you speak Irish?* is correct, though *Gaelic* can also be used. The Irish language is really the same language—with dialectal differences—as Scots Gaelic is and Manx Gaelic (or just *Manx*) used to be.

ESCALATE, as in *prices are escalating*, is a cliché-word.

ESCORT, meaning 'person accompanying a girl to a dance', or the like. Non-U. But agencies who supply them call them that.

ESTABLISHMENT: This celebrated word, whose origin in the sense as in *The Establishment*, is in some doubt, is to-day extremely jargon.

EUPHORIC, as in *I'm feeling very euphoric this morning*, deriving from Medicine, has, in general use, become jargon. The corresponding abstract noun, *euphoria*, is not so widely used.

EVEN: *Even Steven*, meaning 'fifty-fifty'. Cliché-slang.

EVENING: *evening meal*; see MEAL.

EVER: *I'm ever so glad to see you*. Non-U. *Never ever*; see NEVER.

EXCESS: *In excess of* is a cliché-expression—*It will cost in excess of five pounds*.

EXCLUSIVE; see CLIQUY.

EXCUSE: *Excuse me!* is, in most uses, non-U. (*Excuse me, I didn't quite catch what you said.*) Possibly the U also say it on some occasions, as, for instance, if brushing by someone in

49

a passage. *Please, miss, may I go to the excuse?*, meaning 'the lavatory', was once used by non-U (? working-class) children and perhaps still is. *Excuse my glove*; see GLOVE.

EXPECT: *She's expecting* (i.e. a baby) is a well-known non-U phrase. Just after she's had the baby *She's as well as can be expected* is much said. But this expression is also used outside this context, as, for instance, of someone recovering from the effects of an accident.

EXPERT: *He's an expert*—in something (say, Aerodynamics). This word is much used by the General Public. If you are an expert, the use is very annoying.

EXPLORE: *explore every avenue*; see AVENUE.

EXPONENTIALLY, as in *the price is increasing exponentially*, meaning 'very much', is a mathematical term which is used by journalists and has spread to others. Most of those who use it are in fact not able to expand e^x in terms of x.

EXTRAPOLATE: This word, which derives from Mathematics, has become a piece of much-used jargon applied to non-mathematical things—*to extrapolate from a situation*. The true mathematical sense is probably not quite appreciated by most of those who use the word and, oddly enough, the much more common Mathematical antonym, *interpolate*, is not used by the General Public.

EYE: *I could hardly believe my eyes* is a cliché.

FAB: This rather modern word is often used by others than the young, but, then, usually in inverted commas.

FACE, noun: *Was my face red!*; see RED.

FACE, verb: *Let's face it*—as in "You've made an awful mess of things, let's face it". Much used by the non-U. It is no better when expanded to *Let us face it* as the *Sunday Times* printed it recently.

FACT: *I know for a fact that* . . . is a cliché. Often the user does not know it for a fact. *In actual fact* and *in point of fact* are clichés. *The fact of the matter is* . . . ; see MATTER.

FAIR: "*A*. Well then I'll meet you at three.—*B*. Fair enough." Cliché, very popular with the non-U.

FAMILY: *Have you any family?*, meaning wife and/or child or children, is non-U. *She's going to have a family*, meaning 'a baby', may still be heard among them.

FANCY: *Fancy that!* is used by the non-U to express surprise at a statement. They can also use the word as in *Just fancy, I met Mr. Smith the other day.*

FANTASTIC: "*A*. So I drove from London to Oxford in an hour.—*B*. Fantastic!" A much overdone interjection.

FAR: Both *As far as in me lies* and *Far be it from me to* . . . are clichés. So is *few and far between.*

FARE: *You might go further and fare worse* is a cliché.

FASCINATING: As an interjection this is much used by the non-U: "*A*. He then gave us a short talk on the Roman occupation of Dacia.—*B*. Fascinating, I'm sure"— meaning that it was *not* fascinating. Indeed the non-U often use the word in the same way as the U use *Really!* (q.v.).

FAST: *fast operator*; see OPERATOR.

FAULT: *You can't fault him* used as, for instance, in the review of a book. Overdone expression.

FEAR: *Without fear or favour* is a cliché.

FEASIBLE: It is well known that it is "incorrect" to use this word in the meaning 'possible', as is frequently done—*It is feasible that he will come to-morrow.*

FEED: The American use of this verb is often to be heard in this country—*they fed the animals corn.* "Come fed!" has been heard in invitations to things like Bridge parties. The expression means 'come, having had your dinner'. It is not so much non-U, as stingy.

FELLOW: This is used by the working class to mean 'a male' —*Why, it's a fella* (so pronounced). The U still use the word as in *I met a fellow at the Club*—but this is perhaps rather old-fashioned.

FERN: This is non-U Scots for *bracken—Isn't the fern lovely?* Oddly enough, the word is not used by the non-U in Wales, where there is also plenty of bracken.

FEW: *few and far between*; see FAR.

FIDDLE, noun, meaning 'a piece of financial sharp practice'. An overdone word.

FIGURE: *He's good at figures,* i.e. arithmetic, is uneducated and may indeed be working-class.

FILLING: Fifty years ago apropos teeth a *stopping* was the U word and *filling* had a slightly non-U effect. Now *filling* is universal.

FINE!, as in "*A.* Then I'll come at two.—*B.* Fine!" Some people use this word to excess. *Not to put too fine a point on it*; see POINT.

FINGER: *Take your finger out!* The exact meaning of this well-known expression is not clear, though it is certainly indecent. It is a cliché. So also is *You can't put your finger on it.* The expression "Keep your fingers crossed" is much overdone.

FIRE: *mend the fire*; see MEND.

FIRST: *First and foremost* is a cliché.

FISH: *He has other fish to fry.* Cliché.

FIT: *survival of the fittest*; see SURVIVAL.

FIX as in *I'll fix it.* This americanism seems fairly harmless.

FIZZ, meaning 'champagne'. If this word ever was U, it became nouveau riche. It now seems to be obsolescent.

FLAKE in *flake out* meaning 'to lose consciousness'. Rather overdone slang.

FLAMING: This word—and also *flipping*—are much used on television as mild, euphemistic swear-words. They are also used by children.

FLAP, noun, meaning 'fuss'—as in *Don't get in such a flap* or *There's a big flap on to-night*. Overworked slang.

FLAUNT is used by the uneducated instead of *flout*—that *would be flaunting the regulations*.

FLEAPIT meaning 'cinema in poor condition'. This slang expression is now obsolete, no doubt because fleas are.

FLIPPING: see FLAMING.

FLU: Essentially non-U for U *influenza*.

FLUFF, as in *He's fluffed it*, for instance of a stroke in a game. Harmless slang.

FLY: *Fly in*—as in *Miss Smith flew in to Birmingham this evening*—is journalese.

FOLD, verb, meaning 'to cease, to pack it in' as in *Smith and Company have folded*. Much overdone. Possibly to say *I'll fold* at Poker, meaning 'I'll pass out', is harmless.

FOLK: This is an affected word, used by simple-lifers and the like—*See what the folk will have to drink* or *Well, folk, what will you have to drink?* "Carriage folk"; see CARRIAGE.

FOLLOW: *I follow* meaning 'I've understood what you've said' is non-U.

FOOT: *Take the weight off your feet*, meaning 'sit down', is a cliché, and essentially non-U. So is *He didn't put a foot wrong*.

FORCE: *He's a force to be reckoned with*. Cliché.

FOREMOST: *first and foremost*; see FIRST.

FORENAME: This is the American for *Christian name* and is now often used in this country, even on forms.

FORESEEABLE: *In the foreseeable future*; see FUTURE.

FORGATHER: *We'll forgather at the Plough and Harrow, then.* Affected.

FORM: *in any shape or form*; see SHAPE. *Cracking form*; see CRACKING.

FOURPENNY: *A fourpenny one* meaning 'a hard blow' seems to be vulgar. The origin of the expression is not known.

FRANKLY, as in "*A*. Do you like avocado pears?—*B*. Frankly, no." Grossly overworked; some speakers interlard their conversation with the word.

FREE: *Free, gratis and for nothing* is a cliché. So also is *Free, white and twenty-one*. This, originally American, saying is presumably taboo to-day. *For free*, see p. 11.

FRENCH FRIED is felt by restaurant-keepers to be U-er than *chips*. But is it?

FRIEND: *My friend* meaning 'my boy-friend' is much used by non-U girls, and, no doubt, by non-U homosexual men. There is a curious use of *friend* as in *Some of my best friends are Germans*. This means that the speaker really has a prejudice against Germans, but imagines himself a model of tolerance. The very fact of saying it does however discriminate against the Germans.

FRINGE: *Fringe benefit* is a cliché.

FROST, meaning 'flop' or the like, as in *Smith's party was an awful frost*. Old-fashioned slang.

FROZEN: *frozen to the marrow*; see MARROW.

FRUSTRATED, as in *It does make you feel a bit frustrated* or *frustrating* as in *It's a bit frustrating*. These are jargon words, deriving from Psychology.

FRY: *to have other fish to fry*; see FISH.

FUN, adjective, as in *It's a fun thing to do*. A fairly recent americanism. *Good clean fun*; see CLEAN.

FUNNY: *Funny peculiar* has been overworked.

FURY: *Sound and fury signifying nothing*; see SOUND.

FUTURE: *In the foreseeable future* is a cliché.

FUZZ: *The Fuzz*, meaning 'The Police', is now much used, no doubt by all classes.

GARTER: *I'll have your guts for garters*; see GUT.

GEE, GEE-GEE, as in *He lost a packet on the gee-gees*. Old-fashioned slang.

GEE!: American exclamation (euphemism for *Jesus!*). Still perhaps used by English schoolboys.

GEEZER, as in *an old geezer*. This harmless American slang-word still has a certain currency in England.

GENIUS: This word is applied by the uneducated in a very overrating manner to someone good at some academic subject. A scholar to whom it is so applied, and who, in his own opinion, does not deserve the epithet, is likely to be annoyed by it.

GENTLEFOLK: They're *gentlefolk* meaning 'they're U', is an expression once used by the U. It can hardly be heard to-day.

GENTLEMAN: *Is he a gentleman?*, meaning 'Is he U?', was once standard talk among the U, but the use seems to be dying out. The non-U use *gentleman* where the U would say *man*—*A gentleman on the bus told me . . .* or *He seems a very nice gentleman*. The phrase *Be a little gentleman* was once

55

used to naughty little boys (probably by the non-U). *Is he a gentleman?*, of a dog, meaning *Is he male?* was a one-time female expression. No doubt it arose because *bitch* could hardly be used, *lady-dog* being the term—hence its opposite *gentleman-dog*.

GEOGRAPHY: *Let me show you the geography of the house*, a one-time U expression, probably dead to-day, meaning 'let me show you where the lavatory is'.

GET, noun: Term of abuse rather similar to *bastard*. A working-class expression, popularised on television.

GET, verb: *It's got to be good* or *It had better be good* (as, for instance, of an excuse). Overworked. *Get off it!* is used by the non-U in much the same way as *You must be joking!* (see JOKE, verb).

GHASTLY: A one-time vogue word among the U—*I feel positively ghastly this morning* or *What a ghastly hat.* It can still be heard.

GIFT: Non-U as against U *present. Gift-wrapping, gift-wrapped* are used by shops. The term *gift-shop*, for instance, at an airport, is standard.

GIGGLE, noun: *I just did it for a giggle* or *It was rather a giggle.* Non-U, perhaps even working-class, though, no doubt, it can be used by members of other classes in inverted commas.

GIRL: *glamour-girl*; see GLAMOUR. *Little girls' room*; see ROOM.

GIVE: *What gives?*, meaning, essentially, 'What's going on?' is an American expression, translated from German *was gibt es?* of the same meaning. It can be heard in England too. *Do give over!*, meaning 'Stop it!', said, for instance, to a child, was (is?) working-class. *I give up!* as in "*A.* I'm afraid I still don't understand what Osmosis really is.—*B.* I give up!", meaning that, exasperated, he can do no more by way of explaining. Non-U.

GLAMOUR: *glamour girl*, an expression of the nineteen-twenties, now no longer heard.

GLASSES: see SPECTACLES.

GLOVE: *Excuse my glove!* A non-U expression, once used when shaking hands with gloves on. Perhaps still in use?

GLUTTON: *He's a glutton for punishment.* Harmless cliché.

GO: *to go further and fare worse*; see FARE. *Go on the bed*; see BED.

GOD!: This exclamation was, of course, once a little frowned upon. Now it is considered harmless, though many people find annoying a continued repetition of it throughout a whole conversation. *God bless!* is used by the non-U when drinking.

GOOD: *Good!* is used in a tiresome way by some expositors, meaning, essentially 'You have understood correctly'. "*A.* You then differentiate.—*B.* Oh, I see, $x^2+2x=a^2$—*A.* Good!" With one celebrated mathematician I always felt that he would one day say "Two plus two equals four", to be followed by my assent and his "Good!". *That ought to do Smith a piece of no good.* Cliché-slang. *Good health!*, *good luck!*; see CHEERS; *good egg*; see EGG; *good grief!*; see GRIEF; *your good lady*; see LADY; *a good time was had by all*; see TIME; *My good man*; see MAN.

GOOD-BYE: *Good-bye now* is a non-U way of saying good-bye.

GOOD-OH!: "*A.* I've got some chocolate—*B.* Good-oh!" This Australian expression came to be used in this country in inverted commas, probably with the realisation that it was Australian. It is now fairly general.

GOODY, noun: *Goodies*, as in *a basket of goodies*, is slightly affected. The exclamation *Oh, goody!* is affected female.

GOVERNOR: *The Governor*; see p. 9.

GOWN: This is non-U for U *frock* or *dress*. But in technical use —in dressmaking circles—*gown* is no doubt correct.

GRAND: This used to be used, certainly by the non-U, possibly also by the U, of people of high social status. *The Alfonso-Smiths are very grand.* It may still be used in a somewhat similar manner, as in "*A.* I'm going to lunch at the Palace.—*B.* How very grand!"

GRANTED: An expression used by the non-U when someone says *Pardon!* (q.v.) to them.

GRASS ROOTS: Used to describe the rank-and-file of the electorate, this was originally American. In England, it has become something of a cliché.

GRATIS: *free gratis and for nothing*; see FREE.

GREAT: *That's great!* Cliché-expression, either used genuinely ("*A.* My son's just got a First at Oxford.—*B.* That's great!") or sarcastically ("*A. And* it's going to rain.—*B.* That's great!).

GREATCOAT: see TOPCOAT.

GREEN, noun. It is non-U to refer to a *green* at Croquet (instead of a *lawn* or *court*).

GREENS: When eating, this is non-U for cabbage and the like.

GRIEF!: *Good grief!* is an exclamation, used in comics because it is harmless and not-swearing. It has achieved a certain currency in actual speech.

GRIND: *to have no axe to grind*; see AXE. *To grind to a halt*; see HALT.

GROOVY: This fairly modern word is used naturally by the young, and by most others in inverted commas.

GROTTY: This slang word can, in most usages, be replaced by the more normal (and U) *wretched—A grotty sort of place.*

GROVEL: *I grovel!*, i.e. in apology, used once to be quite considerably used by the affected.

GROWTH: This is the almost universal euphemism for *tumour.* The word is naturally disliked by those who dislike euphemisms. In the mind of the General Public it carries with it an implication of malignancy and certain death. This is a pity, because some tumours are benign and not all malignant tumours constitute a death-sentence.

GUEST: This is the word by which hotels refer to the customers. The sign *overnight guests* can often be seen on small boarding-houses, etc.; it means *bed and breakfast* (for which the abbreviation *b. and b.* is still used in advertisements). But a guest who has to pay is surely a misnomer. The U realise this in their expression *P.G. =paying guest,* a term still in use. (It can be employed as a verb—*I was peegeeing it in Budleigh Salterton.*) The expression *Be my guest!* is used by the non-U, on occasions such as that on which someone wants to use your telephone.

GUM-BOOT: see WELLINGTON.

GUTS: This is a very popular word, both literally (*an awful guts-ache*) or, more commonly, figuratively (*put some guts into it!*). But many people find the word unpleasant, except, of course, when used technically (*the blind gut*). There is a particularly unpleasant expression, much used on television as in "If you do that again, I'll have your guts for garters".

GUV: This is used by the working classes (particularly Cockneys) in situations in which they used to say *Sir*; they evidently do not like the latter word with its connotation of subservience. As from a taxi-driver to his fare—*Where d'you want to go, guv?*

GUY meaning 'man'—*he's a nice guy.* This American use is often to be met with in England. *Guys and dolls*; see LAD.

HAG: This word was (? is) much used by the female U—"I look a positive *hag* this morning".

HALF: *My better half* is facetious non-U for 'My wife'. In telling the time the non-U often say *half four* to mean 'four-thirty' instead of the normal *half past four*. This is very confusing to visiting Germans, who, when they say *halb vier*, mean 'three thirty'. *Half after four* is also much used on the wireless.

HALT: *To grind to a halt* is a cliché.

HAND: *my hand hasn't lost its cunning*; see CUNNING.

HANDBAG (woman's) is non-U against U *bag*.

HANDLE: *A handle to his name*, meaning 'a title', is rather old-fashioned non-U.

HANG: *thereby hangs a tale*; see TALE.

HAPPEN: *Happen it will*, meaning 'perhaps', is used on television to indicate that the speaker is using dialect. The phrase does actually exist in the dialects. The use of the word as in *It's all happening in the Midlands* is a cliché.

HAPPY: *Are you quite happy about . . .* is a cliché . *Are you happy in your work?* is an overdone joke.

HARD: *hard of hearing*; see HEARING; *a long hard look*; see LOOK.

HARDWARE is a piece of scientific slang, now much loved by the General Public. It is applied, for instance, to computers and rockets, and means the actual object as opposed to the theory behind it.

HARRY: There was a curious, cliché use of this name in the nineteen-fifties, as, for instance, to a child: "If you do that again, it'll be Harry Smackers for you". The use, no doubt non-U, seems dead now.

HAT: "I am now wearing my Vice-Chancellor's hat"; meaning 'I am now speaking in my rôle as Vice-Chancellor'. The idea of the two (or more) hats has become a cliché, very popular in both pompous speech and journalese.

HATE: *I hate to mention it*; see MENTION.

HAVE: According to television the Police are liable to say *Let's be having you!* when they arrest you. Do they actually say this? *Or what have you* is a rather non-U cliché used exactly like *or whatever* (q.v.).

HEAD, meaning 'headache'—*I've got an awful head*—was certainly once U. It is doubtful how far—if at all—the use persists. The American *head-cold* is much used in this country; the English for it is just *a cold*—*a cold in the head* is old-fashioned. *You'd better get your head down*, meaning 'You'd better have a sleep'; this Service use is now cliché-slang and rather non-U. *Hit the nail on the head*; see NAIL; *keep a civil tongue in one's head*; see TONGUE.

HEALTH: *Good health!*; see CHEERS; *the temple of health*; see TEMPLE.

HEAP applied to a car—*that old heap*—is a rather overdone piece of slang.

HEAR: *You heard!* as in "*A*. Move your bloody car out of *my* parking-place.—*B*. [No response]—*A*. You heard!" is non-U cliché-slang.

HEARING: *hard of hearing* meaning 'deaf' is a cliché.

HEART: *dicky heart*; see DICKY.

HEATH: *On one's native heath*, as in *A fine example of a Postmaster-general on his native heath*. Cliché.

HEAVE-HO: *They gave him the old heave-ho*, meaning 'they sacked him'. Cliché-slang, probably non-U, now not much used.

HEEL, meaning 'a contemptible man', or the like—*Sorry I was such a heel*. This American use may be met with in this country.

HELP: *Can I help you?* is non-U; its main use is as said by a shop-girl to a customer entering the shop. *Help yourself!*, as to someone asking to use another person's telephone or box of matches, is also non-U.

HERE: *It's what we're here for* is used, in a manner intended perhaps as ingratiating, to acknowledge thanks for some service rendered.

HIGH: *high tea*; see TEA.

HOLD: *Hold it!* meaning 'stop!' is rather overdone slang.

HOLIDAY: *on holiday*; see p. 11.

HOME: This is non-U as against U *house* in, for instance, *They've a lovely home.* The phrase *She's not at home* used to be (still is?) said by servants to indicate that their mistress does not wish to receive that particular visitor; for him to reply, as has been done, *But I saw her through the window*, is a gaffe. *His spiritual home is Germany* is a cliché.

HOMERIC: *Homeric laughter*; see LAUGHTER.

HOMEWORK: *To do one's homework*, indicating that one has come prepared for the meeting, or the like, is a cliché much-used in ministerial, official and Service circles.

HONESTLY: *Quite honestly, I don't much like that kind of play.* Used thus, the word is a cliché.

HOO-HA, meaning 'fuss'—*all that hoo-ha*—is cliché-slang.

HOPE: *I devoutly hope*; see DEVOUTLY.

HOPEFULLY, meaning 'I hope'—*Hopefully, I shall arrive about four*—is an americanism; it is a translation of German *hoffentlich*. It is much used in England, and many people find it very annoying. Some new words have apparently been modelled on *hopefully*. "Thankfully, he didn't owe *me* any money" (i.e. 'I'm glad to say'); and "It all looks cautiously promising" (i.e. 'even being cautious, it all looks promising').

HORSE: *Horses for courses*, meaning, for instance, some things are good for one purpose, some for another, is a cliché. The idea is that some horses are good on soft going, others on hard, or the like.

HORSE-RIDING is non-U as against U *riding*. *Horse-back riding* is American.

HOST: *Mine host*, applied, for instance, to the landlord of a pub, is affected.

HOUND: Everyone knows that this word (not *dog*) is used apropos hunting.

HOUSE: *the geography of the house*; see GEOGRAPHY.

HOUSEWIFE: This has become the official designation of married women who have not a job. Presumably Women's Lib finds it derogatory; it is certainly non-U.

HOW: "I thought I had the Jack of Trumps—how silly can you be!" This use is non-U. *How's yourself?*, meaning, essentially, 'How d'you do?', is hearty and/or non-U.

HOW-DO is a way of saying *how d'you do* still used by some non-U. I have heard it used by a U person in inverted commas to a dog (*Say how-do to the lady*).

HUBBY: This is used by the non-U—*My hubby*. The U just say *husband*.

ICEBERG: *It's the tip of the iceberg* is a cliché.

ICE-CREAM: Non-U *I'll have an ice-cream* against U *I'll have an ice*. But the U find it difficult to avoid the word when they buy the stuff in bulk—you can hardly say *I'm going to buy some ices*.

IDEA: *I'll give you a rough idea* is a cliché. *That's the idea!* is non-U; some speakers interlard their conversation with it —"*A.* So I then go down High Street?—*B.* That's the idea!"

IDENTIFY as an intransitive verb—*You've got to identify with the Ugandans*—is a cliché and/or journalese.

IGNORANT: The working-class apparently use this word to mean 'bad-mannered'.

ILK: In its correct use the word is Scotch, as in *Guthrie of that ilk,* meaning Guthrie of Guthrie, in which the second *Guthrie* is a place-name. But the word has been greatly misused, as a non-U cliché, by the English; to them *others of that ilk* means 'others of that kind'.

ILL: see SICK.

ILLEGIT: *She has an illegit* (i.e. an illegitimate baby) seems a harmless piece of slang. The antonym *legit* was (still is?) used of the theatre—it denotes serious drama, as opposed, for instance, to music-hall. The similar use in music—*jazz or legit*—is surely dead.

IMAGE as in *That won't do the firm's image much good.* This fairly recent use of the word is a cliché.

IMAGINE: *Imagine that!* is used by the non-U as a near-variant of their expression *Fancy that!* (q.v.).

IMMEMORIAL: *From time immemorial* is a cliché.

IMPORTANTLY as in "and, most importantly, the Guatemalans do not like the English"—meaning that this is the most important factor in the situation. Journalese.

IMPRESSIVE: *His execution was rather impressive* (of a pianist, or a croquet-player). A somewhat overdone word.

INCLUDE: *Include me out!* A one-time U joke aping the uneducated, which is perhaps not much heard to-day.

INDEED: This word is much overworked; some people punctuate their conversation with it—"*A.* Do you like

64

chocolate?—*B. Yes, indeed*". Some uses of the word are however harmless—*It is indeed a sad state of affairs.*

INDIVIDUAL: *Individual fruit pies* are non-U; they are also not very nice.

INFER: This is much used by the uneducated in cases in which *imply* would be correct: "Are you inferring that I don't know what I'm talking about?"

INFERIORITY: *Inferiority complex* was at one time a piece of jargon recently imported from Psychology. Now everyone knows the term, and it must be reckoned a cliché.

INFINITE: Rather naturally, this word is often used incorrectly to mean 'very large'. As in *The number of stars is infinite*, a statement which cannot possibly be true.

INFRASTRUCTURE: This word, fairly recently imported from Sociology, is jargon.

INJURY: *Mind you don't do yourself an injury*, said, for instance, to someone about to lift a heavy weight, meaning 'Mind you don't rupture yourself', is non-U. Taxi men sometimes say *I don't want to do myself an injury* as an excuse for not lifting heavy luggage. *To add insult to injury*; see INSULT.

INSTANCE: *For instance* is used by some speakers in an overdone fashion to punctuate a whole conversation (in quick speech they are liable to pronounce it *f'r instance*). Hungarians have the same fault with their equivalent expression *példaul*.

INSULT: *To add insult to injury* is a cliché.

INTELLECTUAL: In some circles—and often in the lower newspapers—this is a term of abuse, sometimes accompanied by an epithet (*a long-haired intellectual*). To many, it is very shocking that this should be so.

INTERFERE (sexually) as in *He interfered with the boy*. Old-fashioned journalese.

65

INTIMACY (sexual): Old-fashioned journalese, as in the reporting of divorce cases. Some of its uses were once considered rather funny, e.g. *Intimacy took place in a taxi.*

INVEST: This word is often used in advertising—the start of it may have been the thirties slogan *You buy a car, you invest in a* [then the name of the car]. The prospective purchaser is thus led to believe that there will be something special about his purchase. *Investment* is used similarly.

INVITE, noun: This was once used by the U as a joke; it was what the lower classes were supposed to say. Perhaps they did. The word is not much used to-day.

INVOLVE: *I don't want to get involved* is almost a cliché. It is often said by witnesses to a motor-accident.

IRANIAN is now official for *Persian*. But many people still use the latter and it is always used of the language—*Do you speak Iranian?* would be impossible.

IT: "This is *it!*" is a cliché used by many different people on many different occasions. As for instance, at a crucial point in a game, or when the time has come to say good-bye to someone—perhaps when the train carrying the person starts to move. But the phrase *This is it* is used by the non-U in quite a different sense—they put it on the door of the lavatory.

JACK is non-U against U *knave* at cards. " 'He calls the knaves, Jacks, this boy!' said Estelle with disdain"— *Great Expectations.* So, to open a jackpot, a U player needs at least a pair of knaves.

JACKET: *Jacket potatoes* is a fairly recent non-U (and restaurant) expression for U *baked potatoes*.

JACQUERIE: *The jacquerie* may appropriately be used by affected U speakers of bodies such as demonstrating students or striking miners.

JAPE, meaning 'a joke', particularly perhaps a practical one, is now old-fashioned slang.

JAR: *Shall we go and have a jar?*, i.e. a pint or half-pint of beer. Rather hearty.

JERRY, meaning 'chamber-pot'. An old U word for this; it has now died out because the thing itself nearly has.

JET: *The jet set* is a term popularised by the lower newspapers and applied to certain younger people. But it is very difficult to know exactly to whom the term does, in practice, apply.

JOB: *Just the job!*, a phrase which, really, does little more than express approval: "So I can stay the night with you here and then go on to London in the morning. Just the job!" Cliché-slang. *Jobs for the boys* is a cliché. So is *job of work*—"Well, it's a job of work".

JOKE, noun: *sick joke*; see SICK.

JOKE, verb: *You must be joking!* A cliché, essentially non-U, used very frequently. "*A.* Lend me a fiver.—*B.* You must be joking!"

JOURNAL; see PERIODICAL.

JOVE: *By Jove!* An old-fashioned U exclamation, often used in writing to typify a certain type of young U speaker.

JOY: *No joy!*, as in "*A.* Were you able to get that special spanner?—*B.* No joy!", i.e. no success. Rather outdated cliché-slang.

JUICE meaning 'petrol'—*to run out of juice*. This fairly harmless piece of slang may now be dead.

KEEP: *Keep out!*; see OUT.

KID: *Kids* meaning 'children' is non-U. So also is *kiddies*— *The kiddies love it.*

KILLING: *How killing!* is a phrase used by elderly U women as a somewhat bored response to an anecdote or the like. *How too killing!* seems to have died out.

KIN: *kith and kin*; see KITH.

KIND: *of any sort or kind*; see SORT.

KINDLY: This is often used by the non-U instead of *Please*— *Kindly shut the door after you.*

KING: *King-size* of, for instance, beds or cigarettes, is essentially an advertising and possibly journalese expression.

KINSMAN: If you are Scotch U, it is permissible to use this word in the sense of 'male relation'.

KIP: *To have a kip*, meaning 'to have a short sleep'. This working-class expression has "caught on" and is frequently to be heard in inverted commas and, of course, on the television.

KITH: *Our own kith and kin.* A cliché, which recently came into prominence in connection with Rhodesia—the white Rhodesians were frequently stated to be this.

KNICKERS: This is fairly widely used as a denying exclamation —"*A.* If you don't hurry up, you'll miss the train—*B.* Oh, knickers!"—and as a graffito. The reason for this latter use is obscure, for, in 1973, the word cannot possibly be considered indecent.

KNOTTY: *A knotty point* is a cliché.

KNOW: There are several very well-known non-U uses of this verb. Namely, *I wouldn't know*, meaning 'I don't know'; also *He didn't want to know*, meaning that he took no interest in what I said. And *You know* tacked on to almost any negative expression, as, for instance, "*A.* Eight twenty-

68

nines are 222, aren't they?—*B*. They're not, you know".
There is a non-U emphatic use, as in *How I ever got home
I do not know* (or, *I simply do not know*). *Not knowing can't say*
is a facetious cliché. *You know what you can do with it*; see DO.
I know for a fact; see FACT.

KNOW-HOW, noun, has become a jargon word.

LAD is often used to give an impression of a warm-hearted,
rather dialect speaker—*Well, lad, what are we going to do
now?*, or *He's only a lad.* The U sometimes use it facetiously
—*What's the lad want?* Hotels seem bored with putting up
the normal signs *Ladies* and *Gentlemen* to indicate the
lavatories, and vulgar hotels have adopted a variety of
alternatives, of which *Lads* and *Lassies* is one. Two others
are *Adam* and *Eve*, and *Guys* and *Dolls*.

LA-DI-DA: An expression used by the non-U to designate
someone (usually a young man) whom they think not
only U but also affected. Often applied to speech.

LADY: *Is Mrs. Smith a lady?*, meaning 'of good birth', once
used by the U, is hardly to be heard to-day. *A lady I met
on the bus* is essentially non-U, though the U equivalent,
woman, always sounds rather impolite. *Your lady wife* is
facetious and refined. *Your good lady* meaning 'your wife' is
often to be heard; it is rather non-U. *His young lady*,
meaning 'his fiancée', once non-U, is surely almost, if not
quite, dead to-day.

LANGUAGE!: i.e. Bad language, meaning 'stop swearing', is
a non-U remark addressed to a man swearing in the
presence of women.

LARGE: *by and large*; see BY.

LAUGH: "So he fell off his cycle—we had to laugh", or "You'd have died laughing". Non-U expressions. *Laugh like a drain*; see DRAIN.

LAUGHTER: *Homeric laughter* is a cliché, often to be found in novels.

LAW: *The Law* is apparently criminal and working-class slang for 'The Police'. It is often to be heard on television. *The Law is an ass* is a cliché from *Oliver Twist. Law of Averages*; see AVERAGE.

LAY: *Lay on, Macduff*; see MACDUFF.

LEADING: "*A*. Who were you out with last night?—*B*. That's a leading question"—meaning that that is what used to be called a *home question* (like a *home truth*). But this is not what a leading question is. The expression is often misused thus.

LEAF: *To take a leaf out of someone's book* is a cliché.

LEAN: "I leant over backwards to understand his side of the case." Cliché.

LEAP, meaning 'to jump' is still used by the Irish peasantry, perhaps by other Irish also. *The horse is a good lepper* is known in England as a facetious remark.

LEARNED is sometimes regarded by the non-intellectual as indicating conceit on the part of the speaker—*My next book is a learned one*. But this would be merely a correct description.

LEAVE: *Leave it with me* is a cliché used by shop-keepers, garage-hands and the like. *To leave no stone unturned*; see STONE. *To leave much to be desired*; see DESIRE.

LEGION: *Their name is legion* is a cliché.

LEGIT; see ILLEGIT.

LEND, noun: *Can I have a lend of your pencil?* is uneducated and working-class.

70

LESS: *Less than*, as in *The author is less than fair to Napoleon* meaning, essentially, that he is *not* fair, is a much-used journalistic turn of phrase.

LIBERTY: *This is Liberty Hall*, said, for instance, when someone comes to stay, is non-U. The meaning is intended to be 'you can do as you like here' but the use of the expression is not always sincere.

LIE, noun: "So I went to London last Monday—No, I tell a lie [*or* I'm a liar], it was Tuesday." A very frequent non-U expression.

LIE, verb: The strong verb *lie* (*I lay, I have lain*) and the weak verb *lay* (*I laid, I have laid*) are confused by the uneducated to a considerable extent, as in *Why don't you just lay on the bed* (i.e. have a rest), instead of the correct *lie. As far as in me lies*; see FAR.

LIFE: *He was the life and soul of the party* is a cliché.

LIGHT: *to shed light on the subject*; see SUBJECT.

LIGHT-YEAR: This is used by the uneducated as a measure of time—*It was light-years ago*. But a light-year is a measure of distance, not time, for it is the distance light travels in a year, going at a speed of about 186,000 miles a second.

LIKE, conjunction; see p. 12.

LIKELY, as in *He'll likely be there to-morrow* is used on television to indicate that dialect is being spoken. In fact the use does occur in the dialects.

LIKING: *Is the steak to your liking?* Non-U.

-LINE: In jargon, this can be used as a meaningless suffix—*storyline*, meaning 'story', and *scoreline*, meaning 'score' (at a match).

LINGO: *Do you speak the lingo?* is a Colonel Blimpish kind of remark. It sounds less uneducated when applied to an Australian aboriginal language than when applied, for instance, to Italian, as it frequently is.

LINGUIST: In England this means a person who speaks several foreign languages. In America it often means a specialist in Linguistics—this kind of person still tends to be called a *philologist* in England. The American use is coming into England, which can cause considerable confusion.

LITERALLY: This word can be heard in use in a manner which is really nonsensical—"I was so angry, I literally went up in smoke".

LITTLE: *little man*; see MAN; *little me*; see ME; *room for a little one?* and *Little girls' room*; see ROOM; *little woman*; see WOMAN.

LIVE: *Where does the soap live?*, meaning, 'where is it kept', is a female remark, giving a rather affected impression.

LOAF: *Use your loaf!*, meaning 'Think!' is often used and seems quite harmless. (*Loaf=loaf of bread*, rhyming slang for *head*.)

LOAN, verb: *Can you loan me your car?* Perhaps rather uneducated.

LOCAL: *The locals*, meaning 'the inhabitants of this place', as in *The locals won't like it*, may be heard among the U. *My local*, meaning the pub where I customarily drink, or, similarly, *the local*, is rather affected.

LOLLY, meaning 'money', was originally a lower-class word. It has been much used in inverted commas and is often to be heard on television.

LONG: *long time no see*; see SEE; *a long hard look*; see LOOK.

LOO, meaning 'lavatory'. One of the most discussed words in the English language. It is now the universal word for the thing, except that elderly U people do not use it. The word came in during the last War and its origin remains totally obscure. Euston station has a *super-loo*.

LOOK: *To take a long hard look* at something is a cliché. *Let's take a look at* . . . as it might be, the weather, is a cliché much used by broadcasters.

LOOK! as in *Look, I can't come to-morrow*. This is really cliché-slang; some speakers use it before very many sentences.

LORDSHIP: *His Lordship* is used facetiously by the non-U to designate either "The Boss" or a la-di-da (q.v.) young man.

LOSE: *Get lost!*, as a mild expression of abuse, is cliché-slang, much used by children. *Lose out—We shall lose out on that deal*—is American, but often to be heard in this country.

LOT: *That's your lot*, meaning 'you've had all you're going to have', is non-U. It is used both genuinely (as of things on a shopping list) and figuratively.

LOUD HAILER: This seems to be a fairly recent use instead of *megaphone*.

LOUNGE: This is a non-U person's word for a room in his house. There is perhaps no exact U-equivalent, though *drawing-room* is one in some sort. But to speak of the lounge of a hotel is of course normal.

LOUSY: A very overdone word, used by all classes.

LOVELY: *How lovely!* is used by the non-U as a response— "*A*. I've got eight grandchildren.—*B*. How lovely!" *Lovely grub!* and *lovely lolly* (q.v.) are cliché-slang.

LOW, noun: *A new low, an all-time low*. Clichés.

LUCK. *The best of British luck* is a cliché, and is possibly non-U, which its abbreviation *The best of British* certainly is. *Good luck*: see CHEERS.

LUMBERED: *and so I'll be lumbered with you*. Working-class, popularised by the television. Also *I'm in lumber*, meaning 'I'm in trouble'.

LUNATIC *Asylum*; see ASYLUM.

LUNCH: This is what the non-U often call what they have at eleven o'clock in the morning. (It is quite reasonable of

73

them to do this, for what the U call *lunch*, the non-U call *dinner*, so to the non-U there is no confusion.) The U have no equivalent expression, for *elevenses* is also non-U. The long periphrasis *coffee-in-the-middle-of-the-morning* is often used by them.

LUNCHEON is still used by very old U-people, also, occasionally, by affected young ones. It is still normal in formal invitations.

MA: This is a non-U thing to call one's mother. There is however little of class-distinction to be seen in the other designations of 'mother'; *Mummy, Mum and Mother* are used by members of all classes. *Mamma* is rare nowadays; the expression *my mamma* is rather affected.

MAC: The use of this as a term of address (to someone whose name does not begin with *Mac*), as in, *Don't do that, Mac!*, is American.

MAC is a harmless abbreviation of *macintosh*.

MACDUFF: *Lay on, Macduff!* Facetious cliché, once much used.

MADAM is naturally used in the better shops and hotels. Apart from this, its use is to-day somewhat restricted. Some men (both U and non-U) use it rather offensively to women with whom they are not acquainted—"Excuse me, Madam, you are standing on my foot".

MADAME is used by waiters, sophisticated or would-be sophisticated. Young uncouth English waiters would do better to avoid it.

MADNESS: *that way madness lies* is a cliché, often used facetiously.

74

MAGAZINE; see PERIODICAL.

MAIL meaning 'correspondence' (i.e. letters, parcels, etc.) is American, but is widely used in England to-day. The verb is not in such general use.

MAJORITY: *the silent majority*. Cliché, much used by journalists and politicians. The implication is usually that the silent majority is on the side of the writer/speaker.

MAN: *Little man*, with preceding epithet, is applied by the elderly female U to designate a non-U man: *Smith is such a nice little man, Smith is a stupid little man*. It is also used by exactly the same kind of person in another meaning: *I've found a splendid little man for the car*, i.e. a man running a small garage. *Old man* was once used as a form of address from man to man, or man to boy. If not dead, it is non-U to-day. As further forms of address it may be observed that *My dear man* is rather affected; *My good man* was once used abusively by the U to the working-classes; even in those days, it gave terrible offence, and for a man to use it to another to-day might well invite a blow.

MANAGEMENT: During the last few decades this word has been used, often facetiously, to replace the older cliché *the powers that be* (q.v.), as for instance "Better not walk on the grass, the management won't like it". It has rather a jargon effect.

MANNER: "He ticked him off in no uncertain manner." Cliché. *By no manner of means*; see MEAN.

MANNERS!: This is often said to a dog occupied in some indecent act, or to a child doing something revolting in the middle of a meal. The expression is—perhaps—rather non-U. The non-U sometimes use it in reference to themselves, after they have belched or hiccuped.

MANSION meaning 'big house' is non-U.

MARROW: "I'm frozen to the (very) marrow" is a cliché.

75

MARVELLOUS: "They've sent the wrong part again. Marvellous!" or "Isn't it marvellous?" Cliché-slang.

MASTER is used, chiefly by the non-U, in a derogatory manner, as in "I wonder what Master Smith is up to now" (referring to a man called Smith). *Young Master* is (was?) a non-U term applied to a young man considered *la-di-da* (q.v.), as in the sentence "Young Master's making himself quite at home".

MATER; see p. 9.

MATTER: *the fact of the matter is . . .* is a cliché. *A matter of business*; see BUSINESS. *What seems to be the matter?*; see SEEM.

ME: *Little me*, as in "That's one up to little me", and *Silly me!*, as in "Silly me!, I've done it again" are used by little and/or silly women, not necessarily non-U.

MEAL: *Evening meal* is an expression which has long been accepted as non-U. It can be used without the article— *I'll be late for evening meal.* The fairly recent expression *Don't make a meal of it*, meaning, approximately, 'Don't take it so seriously', is overdone jargon.

MEAN: "What does *that* mean?" with the *that* emphasised is very much used in response to a wide variety of remarks. "*A.* So, you see, I shan't be able to come to your party, after all.—*B.* What does *that* mean?" (*or*, "What's *that* supposed to mean?") It is a cliché. So, too, is *See what I mean?* in the sense 'Have you understood what I've been saying?' Some speakers punctuate a whole conversation with it. It is non-U. *Well, I mean to say* is also a cliché and a conversation filler. So indeed is *I mean*.

MEANINGFUL: A jargon-word, much used by journalists, politicians—particularly perhaps in *meaningful discussions*— and in pseudo-science—*a meaningful distinction*.

MEANS: *By no manner of means* is a cliché: "*A.* So I have to go

76

to London to fetch it?—*B*. By no manner of means; we'll
have it sent here."

MEDIA: *The media* is a fairly recent cliché. It has been heard
as a singular—*the media does* . . .

MEDICAL: *He's a medical*, meaning a medical member of the
staff of a university, is quite acceptable. *Medic* is no doubt
still used of medical students. *I'm a medical man*, meaning
'I'm a doctor', is hardly heard to-day; it was apparently
rather non-U.

MEET: *Pleased to meet you!*, said on being introduced to
someone, is one of the most celebrated non-U-isms. If a U
person really is pleased to meet someone, he may appropriately say "I've been so much looking forward to
meeting you". *To meet up with* is now much used in this
country; it is an americanism.

MEND: *To mend the fire*, i.e. to make it up, is old-fashioned,
possibly non-U.

MENTAL *Hospital*; see ASYLUM.

MENTION: *I hate to mention it, but* . . . and *If you don't mind my
mentioning it* are both non-U clichés.

MERCY: *We must be thankful for small mercies.* Cliché.

MERRY: *and his merry men*, as in "I wonder what treat Mr.
Heath and his merry men have in store for us now",
meaning 'Mr. Heath and those associated with him'.
Cliché, rather non-U.

MESSAGE: *I think he got the message*, meaning 'I think he has
understood the point', or, very frequently, *Got the message?*,
meaning 'Have you understood the point?' Cliché.

MIGRANT: A fairly recent jargon word used instead of
immigrant; the reason for the alteration in use is not entirely
clear.

MIND, noun: *You must be out of your tiny mind!* Cliché. *The
mind boggles*; see BOGGLE.

MIND, verb: *D'you mind?* is a cliché sentence used in a variety of situations. For instance, it could mean *Get out of my way*, and would then sound rather rude. Or it could be used as in "D'you mind? That's *my* taxi". It is essentially non-U. *I don't mind if I do*, in response to an invitation to, for instance, a drink, is now certainly non-U. Curiously, a century ago, it appears to have been U. It frequently appears just as *I don't mind* in the same meaning, 'Yes, please'. *Mind your back*; see BACK. *If you don't mind my mentioning it*; see MENTION.

MINE: *mine host*; see HOST.

MIRROR is non-U for U *looking-glass*, except in compounds such as *driving-mirror*, *shaving-mirror*, or, technically, as in *the mirror of the telescope*, which are perfectly acceptable.

MISS! is a form of address used by the non-U to barmaids, waitresses, telephone-operators and the like.

MISS: *Miss out on* as in *We seem to have missed out on the speech*, though no doubt acceptable in America, is cliché-slang in England.

MISSIS: *The missis* meaning 'my wife' is non-U, indeed working-class. Oddly enough *The Colonel's missis*, or *His missis* is perfectly U, and still much used by elderly Service people.

MISTAKE: *Make no mistake*, as in *I shall come back again, make no mistake about it*, is a cliché.

MISTER, as in *What d'you think you're up to, Mister?*, said to a trespasser, is lower-class and sounds extremely rude. No doubt the lower-class speaker intends it as extremely rude. The non-U have a curious use of *Mister*. "*A*. [in a golf club or the like] I don't think I've met you before.—*B*. Mr. Vincent", where the U person would say "My name's Vincent". There are two other non-U alternatives,

78

namely "The name's Vincent" and "Vincent's the name", the latter being slightly less non-U than the former.

MIX, noun: *The film's a mix of sentimentality and violence.* Cliché-word.

MOCK: The status of the cliché-phrase *Don't mock me!* is not quite clear to me: is it homosexual—or theatrical?

MOMENT: *At this moment of time* is a venerable cliché, still to be heard. *The moment of truth*; see TRUTH.

MONEY: *It's money for old rope*; see ROPE.

MONKEY, as in *Are you trying to make a monkey of me?*, i.e. 'a fool of me'. An angry, non-U, expression.

MONOKINI: This curious, rather new word is a faintly learned joke. A *bikini* gets its name from Bikini, an atoll of the Marshall Islands, where the renowned atomic explosion took place in 1946; the idea, stupid and in poor taste, is that the garment is as startling as a superbomb. A bikini consists of a cache-sexe and a brassière; it thus has *two* parts, and, in the joke, *bi-* is taken as meaning 'two' (as in *bisexual*). A monokini—or topless bikini—consists only of a cache-sexe and thus has only *one* part—and *mono-* means 'one' (as in *monorail*). I have not been able to find out whether the joke started in France or in England.

MORE: *Any more for any more?* is a non-U phrase asking whether anyone at a meal wants a 'second helping'. I suspect the phrase may still be in use.

MOTHER; see MA. *Shall I be mother?*, meaning 'Shall I pour out the tea?' is non-U.

MOTOR, meaning 'motor-car'. This used to be a normal word for the thing, but, in the main, it has now died out, as has also the corresponding verb—*We motored from London to Oxford* is no longer said, *we drove* being usual. But some, rather affected people (mostly young) have resurrected

79

the noun and would say, for instance, *The Cortina is a very good motor* (instead of *car*).

MOTORCYCLE is non-U for U *motorbike*. (Cf. non-U *cycle*/U *bike*).

MUGGINS: This word is used as in the following interchange "*A*. Who's going to do the washing up?—*B*. Muggins here, I suppose"—*B* is referring to himself/herself. The use is both non-U and affected.

MUM, MUMMY; see MA.

MUSICAL: *She's very musical* is not used by intellectuals (among whom many, but not all, musicians are to be reckoned). They would say *She's very fond of music*.

MUST: *It's a must* is a cliché, often used by journalists—*The Castle is a must for those visiting Brecon*.

MY; see p. 10.

NAIL: *You've hit the nail on the head*. Cliché.

NAME, noun: *A handle to his name*; see HANDLE; *their name is legion*; see LEGION.

NAME, verb: *You name it* as in "Hail, sleet, thunder, all kinds of weather; you name it, we've had it". Cliché.

NANNA, *or* NAN is very widely used by the non-U in the sense 'grandmother'. To-day, there is no danger of a child confusing the word with *nanny*, meaning 'nurse', for the non-U, like most of the U, do not have nannies.

NASTY: *He turned out very nasty*, or *a nasty remark*. Non-U.

NATIVE: *on one's native heath*; see HEATH.

NAUGHTY is used in an affected manner for things that are

in fact greatly in excess of this: *It was very naughty of you to forge that cheque.*

NAY, as in "He forgot to do it, nay worse, he didn't even think of doing it". Essentially journalese, but it has been so overworked, both in speech and writing, that it is perhaps rather dying out.

NEED: *Who needs it?*, as in "Linguistics—who needs it?", meaning 'What do we want *that* subject for?' This is an American expression; it is a translation from Yiddish *wer darf es hobn?*, which means, literally, 'who needs to have it?' The expression is now current in England too. *I needed that!*, said after the first drink of the evening, or on the like occasion, is a cliché.

NEGRO: In these days to approve of, or even admit, racial distinction is, for some reason, considered one of the worst of social crimes—much worse, for instance, than violence. This word is, therefore, naturally, taboo.

NEIGHBOUR: *The neighbours* is non-U—and so is the widespread fear of what they will think. U people would like not to have neighbours, but most of them do.

NERVE: The General Public is very keen on nerves. In some cases the consequent linguistic usages are harmless, as in "*A.* I don't know why I missed that shot [at a game].— *B.* It must have been nerves". But "He's ill—something to do with his nerves", implying mental illness, is somewhat uneducated. There is a curious, uneducated point with regard to shingles. The General Public knows that it has something to do with "nerves". So it has—in the sense that the vesicles appear along the lines of distribution of cutaneous nerves. So we get nonsensical remarks such as "I've had shingles rather badly, but then I'm a very nervy sort of person". *She's a bundle of nerves* is a cliché.

NERVOUS: *nervous breakdown*; see BREAKDOWN.

NEVER: *never ever*, as in *I'll never ever see you again*, is non-U. *I'll never never see you again* is however perfectly U.

NEW: *A new low*; see LOW.

NIBS: *His Nibs*, obsolete (? obsolescent) non-U slang for 'the boss', or the like.

NICELY: *I've done very nicely, thank you*, meaning 'I've had enough to eat'. Non-U.

NICKER, meaning 'pound sterling'. Its frequent use in inverted commas is largely due to television.

NIGGER: Like *negro* (q.v.) now a taboo word. Once in Jamaica I unthinkingly said "I've been working like a nigger all the morning". "Here we usually say *Trojan*", someone said.

NIP: *to nip in the bud*; see BUD.

NITTY-GRITTY; see TACK.

NO: *Oh no!* as in "*A*. I've been ill again.—*B*. Oh no!" Non-U, or at least a cliché. *I won't say no*, in response to an invitation (to have a drink or a chocolate, for instance) is a cliché which apparently annoys many people. *Will you have a cup of coffee or no?* (instead of *not*) is not uncommon and seems to be non-U.

NOB: *one of the nobs*. A non-U expression, now probably obsolete.

NOGGIN: *I'll have a noggin*, i.e. some beer. Originally Service slang, and to-day rather affected except when used by Service people.

NONSENSE: *To make a nonsense of something*. Cliché-slang.

NOSE: *Your nose needs attention*. This revolting phrase is of course non-U. *To rub someone's nose in it*, used metaphorically (i.e. to make them eat their words), is almost equally revolting. *Keep your nose clean*, i.e. have nothing to do with some dirty business, is vulgar. *Parson's nose*; see PARSON.

NOSTRIL: *The breath of one's nostrils* is a cliché.

NOSY, as in *Don't be nosy*, is non-U. So also is *Nosy Parker*, occasionally abbreviated to *Parker*.

NOT: *Isn't he?* is of course normal; to say *Is he not?*, as some do, is rather affected.

NOTECASE; see WALLET.

NOTEPAPER: As is well-known, this is non-U as against U *writing-paper*.

NOTHING: *free gratis and for nothing*; see FREE.

NOW: The americanism *as of now* is frequently to be heard in this country too.

NUMBERED: *its days are numbered*; see DAY.

OBLIGED: *Much obliged!* said in response to something done for one, is non-U. The expression may however correctly be used in business-letters—*I should be much obliged if you would send me . . .*

OBVIOUSLY: This word is greatly overworked, especially perhaps by young people.

OCCASION: *on this auspicious occasion*; see AUSPICIOUS.

ODOUR: If the connotation is an unpleasant odour the word is non-U, as against U *smell*.

OF: *I would of come*; see p. 11.

OFF OF; see p. 6.

OFFICE: There is a curious, non-U use of this to mean 'any room in which one works'. Thus some people call their room in a University, their *office*.

O.K.: This is perhaps the one americanism that is tolerated by all English people. The origin of the expression is difficult; the best account of it is the five articles by A. W. Read in the linguistic journal, *American Speech*, vols. 38–39 (1963–64).

OLD: This word as applied to people who are not old is non-U—either to one's friends (*Old Smith made rather a mess of that*), or to public figures (*I thought old Heath did that remarkably well*). The non-U also apply the word to things —*I better get out the old cycle. Old chap*; see CHAP; *old man*; see MAN.

OLDE: *ye olde* —; see YE.

ON: *What's he on about?*, meaning, 'What's he kicking up a fuss about?' is non-U, or even working-class. So is *You're on!*, meaning 'the bargain is accepted', or the like.

ONE, referring to oneself, as in *One would hardly do that*, seems to be more used by men than by women, especially by rather affected men.

OPERATOR: *a fast operator*=*a quick worker* (e.g. with girls). Rather old-fashioned slang and possibly non-U.

OPINION: *Everyone's entitled to their own opinion.* Cliché, often used at the end of slightly acrimonious arguments. To many, it is an annoying cliché, because, manifestly, everyone is not entitled to their own opinion in scientific matters. *Climate of opinion*; see CLIMATE. *Consensus of opinion*; see CONSENSUS.

OPPORTUNITY: *ample opportunity* is a cliché.

OPT: *opt out*, as in *I'll opt out of that*, meaning 'I'll take no part in that', is overworked.

OPTION: *a soft option* designating something easier than other things (as, for instance, at a University, *Sociology is a soft option*). Cliché.

OSMOSIS: This scientific word (from Physics) has become a piece of jargon, much used by journalists with reference to the interpenetration of ideas.

OUGHT, noun, meaning 'zero', is non-U for U *nought*.

OUGHT, verb: *He didn't ought* is a well-known uneducated use. It can often be heard used in inverted commas by educated people.

OUR: see p. 10.

OURS: *of ours*; see p. 9.

OUT!, meaning 'Get out!' is rude and non-U. *Keep out!*, put as a notice in business premises and offices, is thought to be more effective than *No admittance except on business*; it is also much ruder.

OVERALL: This is a cliché-word, often put in when no word is needed—*The overall results are . . .*

OVERNIGHT: *overnight bag*; see BAG; *overnight guests*; see GUEST.

OXFORD: *He's got an Oxford accent.* This phrase is used by the non-U to mean that a speaker has a U pronunciation. To-day it may be considered something of a misnomer, for Oxford is not as U as it used to be.

P for new pence—*Price 6p*—seems to annoy very many people, presumably because of its (mildly) indecent connotation.

PACK, noun, meaning 'packet'. This American use can frequently be heard in this country. It has been encouraged by advertisers and is often applied to cigarettes.

PACK, verb: *pack it in*, meaning 'to stop'. Rather overworked slang.

PAD, meaning where a person lives (flat or room). A fairly modern slang word, used by many in inverted commas.

PADRE, meaning 'clergyman', can still be heard among retired Army people.

PAIN: *Does your foot pain you?* is non-U; the U say *hurt*.

PANIC: *don't panic!*, meaning 'don't lose your head'. Cliché.

PANSY, meaning 'homosexual', once the favourite word for it, is now not much used; *queer* has replaced it.

PANTS: This is widely used, perhaps mostly by the non-U, in its American sense of 'trousers'. Those who have this use must naturally find some other word for what are normally called *pants*; so they say *underpants* (also American), and shops often use this term too. The U for the thing is still *drawers*.

PAPER: *paper tiger*. A cliché-expression much used by journalists.

PARA as in *In your Para 3 you state that . . .* , still correct in reference to official documents.

PARAMETER: This word (from Mathematics) has become jargon. It is used to mean little more than 'factor entering into a situation'.

PARDON: There are various uses, all non-U, to mention here. *Pardon!* or *Beg pardon!* are used after belching or hiccuping; and the former can also be used meaning 'I didn't hear what you said'. *Pardon me!* is used on occasions such as the carrying of a tray through a crowded room.

PARKY: meaning 'cold'—*A bit parky this morning*—is non-U.

PARSON: To say *He's a parson* is derogatory—*clergyman* is the U word. But clergymen do use *parson* of themselves—*I'm a parson*—no doubt in a self-deprecating sort of way. *The parson's nose* for a bit of a chicken is vulgar.

PARTIAL: *Are you partial to lobster mayonnaise?*, meaning 'do you like it?', is non-U. The word is frequently preceded by *rather*—*Yes, I'm rather partial to it*.

PARTNER: Non-U Croquet players refer to their opponent as

86

their *partner*. The word is of course correct of a doubles-partner. In the vocative—*Sorry, partner, I missed it again*—some players find the word annoying.

PARTY: *Working party* is a cliché—of universities and ministries. *The life and soul of the party*; see LIFE; *keep the party clean*; see CLEAN.

PASS, noun: *to sell the pass*, meaning 'to be a traitor to a cause'. A cliché, and few who use it know which pass is referred to. It is in fact Thermopylae, where a Greek betrayed the Pass to the Persians, for a financial reward, in 480 B.C.

PASS, verb: *Pass away, pass on, pass over* are well-known euphemisms for *die*, much disliked by many. *Pass a remark*; see REMARK.

PASSAGE: *I'm only a bird of passage.* Cliché.

PAST: *the dim and distant past.* Still a much-used cliché.

PATER: see p. 9.

PAVVY, meaning a pavilion on a sports ground. This old piece of schoolboy slang may still be used to-day.

PAY: *pay a call*; see CALL.

PEACE: *No peace for the wicked* is a cliché, rather female —*There's still the washing-up to do; no peace for the wicked!*

PEASANT: This used to be employed by the U of people living in this country—*He was only a peasant, you know*. In this sense it is not much heard to-day, but it can still appropriately be applied to people living in other countries—*Bulgarian peasants*.

PENNY: *Pennies*, meaning 'money'—*She hasn't very many pennies*—is very affected. *To cost a pretty penny* is a cliché. *To spend a penny*, meaning 'to go to the lavatory', can still be heard; it is not necessarily non-U.

PERADVENTURE: *Beyond a peradventure* (or *beyond peradventure*)

87

is a pompous expression sometimes used in speeches, particularly political ones.

PERFORM: *When do I perform?*, as, for instance, of a cricketer asking about the batting order. Rather affected.

PERFUME, noun. Non-U as against U *scent*.

PERIOD!, as in "*A*. I can't lend you the money just now.—*B*. All right, you can't lend me the money. Period!" A cliché, much overworked.

PERIODICAL, noun. There are differences in use between this word and its near-synonyms, *journal* and *magazine*. Thus, readers of *Nature*, the most celebrated of the English scientific journals, must have been shocked to see it referred to recently as *Nature Magazine* in the *Sunday Times*. The word *magazine* should not nowadays be applied to anything learned. *Periodical* is the technical word, used in libraries. *The learned journals* is now a rather old-fashioned academic expression.

PERKS: This slang word seems to be dying out.

PERM: The universal use of this word apropos football pools is in fact uneducated, because what the punter sends in in such circumstances is a combination, not a permutation. Thus it is very often the number of ways of choosing eight things out of ten, that is $^{10}c_8 = {}^{10}c_2 = 45$; the corresponding permutation would be $10 \times 9 = 90$. (*Perm* is better-known in another sense; it is used by all classes—and particularly by women—to mean 'permanent wave.')

PEROXIDE: This is widely current in the meaning 'hydrogen peroxide', H_2O_2. (The phrase *peroxide blonde* was at one time used—the substance is a bleacher of hair.) The use is uneducated, for there are many other peroxides, e.g. barium peroxide, BaO_2.

PERSONA: This word, originally a psychological term, is now to be regarded as jargon.

88

PERSONAL is essentially a non-U word. As for instance in *don't be personal* or *that's a personal question*. It is also used by shops as in *personal notepaper* (e.g. perhaps with the initial of your Christian name on it). This last is also called *personalised* by shops.

PERSONALLY: *Personally speaking, I don't like that kind of play.* Used thus, the word is a cliché.

PERSPECTIVE: *Let's get it into the proper perspective* is a cliché.

PERSPIRE is well-known to be a non-U word. If the U say anything, they say *sweat*.

PESTILENTIAL applied to weather—*What pestilential weather!* —is harmless slang.

P.G.: see GUEST.

PHILATELIST, PHILATELY are rather high-falutin' words for *stamp-collector, stamp-collecting*.

PHONE, noun and verb: This is an essentially non-U abbreviation for *telephone*.

PI, adjective, meaning 'sanctimonious' and the like. This schoolboy word may still be heard among the U.

PIANIST: *concert pianist* is either non-U or non-intellectual or both.

PICK: *to pick someone's brains*; see BRAIN.

PICTURE: *picture card* is the non-U for U *court-card*. *The pictures*, meaning 'the cinema', was once working-class; the phrase was taken up by the U and by intellectuals and is still used to-day.

PIDGIN: *That's my pidgin*. A rather old-fashioned cliché. Many people think of it as *That's my pigeon*.

PIE: The non-U usually say *apple pie*, whereas the U say *tart*. But of course *steak-and-kidney pie* is normal. *Chiffon pie*; see CHIFFON.

PIECE, meaning 'article for a newspaper, contribution to a

89

book'—*I've done my piece*—is journalists' and publishers' jargon. *A piece of no good*; see GOOD.

PIG: *Fascist pigs*. This is what many young people of all classes call the Police, quite without justification.

PILOT: *pilot project*, meaning a preliminary try-out of some piece of work. This is jargon.

PIP: *pipped on the post*; see POST.

PIPELINE: *It's in the pipeline*. Cliché.

PLACE: *He's got a big place down in Hertfordshire*, meaning that he owns a house and land there; this can still be heard. It was and is U.

PLANE, meaning 'aeroplane', is probably non-U. As everybody now knows, the more professional word for the thing is *aircraft*.

PLEASE: *Please yourself!* This is a non-U expression, usually used rather offensively—"*A*. Shall I go to London then? —*B*. Please yourself!"

PLEASED: *pleased to meet you*; see MEET.

PLOY, as in *I don't know what ploy he's engaged in just now*. This word is overdone and is, possibly, rather affected.

PLUSH, adjective, meaning 'luxurious', as in *plush surroundings*. This seems a harmless, if somewhat old-fashioned, piece of slang. *Plushy* can also be used in the same sense.

POCKETBOOK: see WALLET.

PO-FACED is a rather modern word much used by intellectuals. Many people find it unpleasant.

POINT, noun: *Not to put too fine a point on it* is a cliché. So is *You've a point there*, which is more recent. *A knotty point*; see KNOTTY.

POINT, verb: To say *Excuse me* (or *my*) *pointing*, when indicating something or somebody, is non-U.

POLARISE: This scientific word (from Optics) has become jargon. It is much used by journalists in a variety of figurative senses. E.g. "An economic system polarised between Capital and Labour"; *or* "Since I talked to him, attitudes have polarised even more".

POPPET as in *she's rather a poppet*. An affected word.

PORTION is non-U against U *helping (a big helping of pudding)*.

POSH: This slang word, which, despite much popular discussion, remains of unknown origin, is used by children of all classes. Many grown-ups use it in inverted commas.

POSITION used as a verb is somewhat jargonish—*the screw is positioned at the back of the plate*.

POST: *He was pipped on the post*. This seems a harmless cliché.

POSTAGE STAMP, as in *Have you a postage stamp?* or *He collects postage stamps*, is non-U. The U just say *stamp*, in both contexts.

POST-LACTARIAN: Curiously, this word still survives. It means 'someone who puts the milk in after the tea'—and is thus U, for the non-U put the milk in first. It must be a Victorian piece of facetiousness; it is not recorded in the *Oxford English Dictionary*.

POST-PRANDIAL: This cliché word is still in facetious use, as in *a post-prandial nap*. It is affected.

POTATO: *jacket potatoes*; see JACKET.

POT-LUCK as in *Come and take pot-luck with us*. Non-U.

POUR: *Shall I pour?*, meaning 'Shall I pour out the tea?', is non-U. The U say nothing in such a context; if they need to refer to the act they say *Shall I pour out the tea?* "May I pour you a drink?" is also essentially non-U.

POWDER: *I'm just going to powder my nose*, a female euphemism for going to the lavatory. Not entirely non-U. *powder room*; see ROOM.

POWER: *the powers that be* is a cliché, still much in use.

PRAY: *pray do!*, as in "*A*. Can I sit down?—*B*. Pray do!" is very affected, but may still be heard, though not among the non-U.

PRE-: This prefix is somewhat misused, as in the direction *To be pre-boiled before use.*

PREGNANT: To-day this is the standard word for the situation in all classes. The word used to be considered rather unpleasant, and some elderly people still find it so.

PREJUDICE: *I'm not prejudiced, but . . .* is a cliché.

PREMIER; see DON.

PRESENT: *present company excepted*; see COMPANY.

PRESENTLY: The American sense of this word—*He is presently in America* (i.e. 'at present')—is gaining ground, particularly in journalese.

PRESERVE is non-U for *jam*. The ancient joke, U young man to son of nouveau riche jam-maker "Does your father preserve?" [i.e. pheasants] has however lost whatever small point it once had.

PRESSURE, verb, is a cliché word, as in "Don't try and pressure me; I'll do it as soon as I can".

PRETTY: *cost a pretty penny*; see PENNY.

PRICY as in *It's rather pricy at the Ritz.* Non-U.

PRINCIPLE: *It's the principle of the thing.* A cliché, still in existence, and still often used in the old way, as when someone points out that they are not taking some action merely for the money.

PRIORITY: *You must get your priorities right* is a cliché.

PROBLEM: *that's no problem*, as in the interchange "*A.* How can I get from Uttoxeter to Wrexham?—*B.* That's no problem". This is a much-used cliché, more in fashion with the non-U than with the U.

PROCEED: This word is used by policemen—*I was proceeding down Coronation Street.*

PROFESSOR: Many people think professors should be called

92

Mr. when addressed. This is wrong. It derives from the fact that, at Oxford and Cambridge, some professors were (? are) correctly called *Mr.* Other professors there are correctly called *Professor*, and so are all professors at other universities. Students at provincial universities use the abbreviation *Prof.*—*Prof. Ross* or *I must go and see the prof.* The uneducated usually misspell the word as *Proffessor* and, on letters, often abbreviate it to *Pro.*

PROJECT, noun, as in *my research project.* This is a jargon word, much used in applying for grants to implement research work. It is also used apropos things children do at school; this last use sounds rather pompous. *Pilot project*; see PILOT.

PROTEST, verb: see p. 12.

PSEUDO, as in *he's awfully pseudo* (i.e. phony). This slang word seems to be dying out.

PUD, meaning 'pudding', as in *What are we having for pud?* or *steak and kidney pud.* This abbreviation, which is not non-U, is grossly overworked.

PULL: *to pull strings*; see STRING.

PUNDIT: *The pundits*, as in *Better ask the pundits*, is an expression used by non-intellectuals. Most of us who are pundits in their sense feel it embarrassing to be referred to by this word.

PUNISHMENT: *a glutton for punishment*; see GLUTTON.

PUT: *Put it like this* (or *that*) is a cliché. "*A.* Was Einstein right?—*B.* Well, put it like this, there *could* be alternative Theories of Relativity."—"If you put it like that, I'll make sure I finish it by to-morrow." *Put the skids under*; see SKID.

QUEER, noun: see PANSY.

QUESTION: *A burning question* is a cliché. So is *good question!*, as in the interchange "*A*. If something travels faster than light, does it arrive before it sets out?—*B*. Good question!" *The 64,000-dollar question*; see DOLLAR.

QUID: *quids in* as in "If you buy that house now for ten thousand, you'll be quids in in five years' time". A vulgar expression.

QUILT is felt by many to be non-U for *eiderdown*.

QUITE: A somewhat affected response to a statement, used more by the U than by the non-U. As in "*A*. But I don't see how I'm ever to get from Uttoxeter to Wrexham.— *B*. Quite!"

QUOTE: *And I quote* is a cliché much used in lectures and speeches; it means that the speaker is about to give the actual words of somebody else.

RADIO: This used to be non-U, except in technical use. The U equivalent was *wireless*. Now *radio* is normal.

R.A.F.: Care should be taken with this abbreviation. It is better for non-service people to say *Royal Air Force* in full. Service people say this too, but use *R.A.F.* or *Air Force* in conversation in which they have already mentioned the the thing in full. *Raf*, pronounced to rhyme with *gaffe*, is non-U and "other ranks".

RAG: *The rag trade*, meaning 'the couturier's business', etc., is a piece of cliché slang which has gained a wider currency than it would otherwise have done because of a television programme of that name. *A red rag to a bull*; see BULL.

RAINCHECK: "I'll have to take a raincheck on your party", meaning 'I won't be able to come to it' is American, but often to be heard in this country.

RAINCOAT: Some find this word non-U, but it is certainly sometimes used by U-speakers.

RASPBERRY as in *They gave us a raspberry* is, like the actual sound, very vulgar.

RAT: *The rat race* is a cliché.

RATHER!: "*A*. Would you like to go to London?—*B*. Rather!" This use is so old-fashioned as hardly to be heard to-day; it was once U.

REACT: "I've written to him and I hope he will react favourably." Such a use of *react* is a cliché, often used in business letters.

READ, noun: "*Treasure Island* is certainly a good read." This is non-U and uneducated, but it has been taken up by reviewers; their use must be considered affected.

READ, verb: *We'll take it as read, shall we then?* Cliché.

REALLY!: This is a response of the elderly female U to a remark that they consider boring. "*A*. I hear James has gone to London.—*B*. Really!" The word has a special intonation, which cannot be indicated in normal printing.

RECALL meaning 'to remember'—as in *I don't recall*—is non-U. Cf. RECOLLECT.

RECAP, short for *recapitulation*, is a jargon word, much used in expounding matters. *We'll have a recap* means essentially 'I'll go through it once again'.

RECEIPT: Old-fashioned U people still use this word in the sense 'recipe'.

RECKON: *a force to be reckoned with*, see FORCE.

RECOLLECT meaning 'to remember'—as in *I can't quite recollect*—is non-U. Cf. RECALL.

RED: *Was my face red!* is a cliché—essentially non-U—used

to describe a situation in which the speaker was in some way put to shame—"I thought the girl next to me was married and asked her how her children were. She was in fact a Miss Smith. Was my face red!" *A red rag to a bull*; see BULL.

REFINED: This word is used by the U to denote certain affected types of non-U pronunciation or behaviour—for instance the pronouncing of *ride* almost as if it was *raid*; or the use of the pronunciation *Moddom* for *Madam* in women's shops. When so used the U often pronounce the word with the second syllable rhyming with *pained* and, sometimes, the word is spelt *refained*.

RELATIVE, noun, is a non-U word, the corresponding U expression being *relation*.

RELAX: *Relaxed*—as in *He seems quite relaxed*—is a jargon-word, like its opposite, *tense* (q.v.). The imperative, *Relax!*—a cliché—is much used, especially to a person being tiresome.

REMARK: *He passed the remark, He made a nasty remark, Don't pass remarks*—all very well-known to be non-U-isms.

REPEAT, as in "I don't like onions, they repeat so", is very non-U.

RESEARCH, noun: An acceptable definition of *research* would perhaps be 'something that is published as a learned book or as an article in a learned journal'. But, to-day, the term is used of the most trivial work and, it is to be supposed, even schoolchildren often conduct research.

RESEARCH, verb: see p. 12.

RESIDENCE: "This is Mr. Smith's residence"—used by butlers on the telephone.

REVEREND: It is non-U to use this to a clergyman as a form of address (as in "Have some more tea, Reverend"). *The Reverend doesn't like toast* and *He is a Reverend* are also non-U.

REVERSE: "*A*. Are you feeling better?—*B*. Very much the reverse." Cliché.

REWARDING is a modern cliché-word used in application to a variety of things (for instance, some task or job).

RIDE: *To go for a ride in a car* is non-U; the U word is still *drive*.

RIGHT is often used as a cliché-word as in "Then you go down High Street, right?" meaning 'Have you understood that?' *That's right* is one of the most frequent non-U ways of saying *Yes*. (The expression can however be used correctly as in "*A*. Nine nineteens are 171, aren't they?—*B*. That's right"—meaning that it really is right.) *How right you are!* is a cliché expressing agreement with someone else's statement—"*A*. That'll cost a lot of money.—*B*. How right you are!" The adjective, as in *He's a right crook, is Charlie*, is working-class.

RIGID: see SHAKE.

RING: In respect of telephones, *ring me* and *ring me back* are non-U, while *ring me up* is U.

RITZY: This americanism is often to be heard in this country.

ROAD: *Any road* meaning 'anyway' interpolated into normal English is widely used by television actors to indicate that dialect is intended. The expression is in fact widespread in the dialects.

ROB: *I've been robbed* as, for instance, of a game which the speaker has lost by a narrow margin. This is an overdone word.

ROOM: *The smallest room* (occasionally, *The small room*) is one of the non-U expressions for 'lavatory'. *Where is the boys' room?*, or *the little girls' room?* is facetious non-U. *Powder room*, used in many English hotels, is American. *Room for a little one?* is a non-U cliché; it is considered especially

97

funny if the person seeking a place is very fat. *Utility room*; see UTILITY.

ROPE: *It's money for old rope*, meaning that it is an easy job. A harmless cliché, still used.

ROTTEN: *rotten to the core*; see CORE.

ROUGH: *a rough idea*; see IDEA.

ROYAL: *Royal Air Force*; see R.A.F.

RUDE meaning 'indecent', once non-U, is now used facetiously by many people and writers.

RUMBLE as in *They've rumbled me* meaning 'They've found out what I'm doing'. Non-U cliché.

RUMPUS-ROOM: This americanism has a certain currency in England now; but many English people do not quite know what the word means.

SACRED applied to religious music or pictures is rather non-intellectual. *Sacred cow* is a well-known piece of jargon.

SAD meaning 'not properly risen', of a cake. This is essentially a dialect word, but is widely used in various provincial forms of standard English (e.g. in Leeds).

SAGA: This word, from Icelandic, is correctly used of a certain type of story, often one dealing with the history of a family (as in the Icelandic Family Sagas). So it is correctly used by Galsworthy in his title *The Forsyte Saga*. But it is often used incorrectly—as when the *Sunday Times* referred recently to "the Beowulf Saga", for the Anglo-Saxon epic poem *Beowulf* is not a saga, or in *The Alf Garnett Saga*, title of a recent film.

SAHIB: *He's not a sahib*, meaning 'He's non-U', is now obsolete. So too is the overdone phrase *a pukka sahib*, meaning someone who behaves like a gentleman.

SANDWICH SPREAD: This expression is non-U, because the nasty substance is itself non-U. But quite good hotels often give it one.

SANGUINARY: This was at one time much used as a facetious euphemism for *bloody*. But this latter word is now perfectly acceptable in print, so *sanguinary* has died out.

SARKY, meaning essentially 'sarcastic'. This schoolboy word continues, and seems harmless.

SAUSAGE in *Not a sausage!*, meaning 'nothing at all'. Much overdone.

SAY: *I would say*, as in "*A*. How much is it going to cost?—*B*. I would say about two hundred pounds", is a cliché, rather non-U. *Having said this . . .* is a cliché. So too, really, is *If I may say so*. *It's not for me to say* is an annoying, rather non-U phrase. It was much used by servants when asked something that they considered a question unsuitable between master and servant. *You can say that again!*, as in "*A*. I'm sorry you lost that money.—*B*. You can say that again!" is a cliché, rather non-U. "I said to Mrs. Smith"; this kind of phrase is a frequent element in the conversation of the female lower class; it is felt to lend verisimilitude. "As I was saying to Mrs. Smith"—if you really were saying it—is less objectionable. *You don't say!* is used by the non-U to express surprise at a statement. *Though I says it as shouldn't*; see SHOULD. *What you are trying to say is . . .* ; see TRY. *Well, I mean to say*; see MEAN.

SCALDED: "I went down the drive like a scalded cat"—or *kitten*. An unpleasant phrase, considerably used.

SCENE: *It's not quite my scene*, meaning 'it's not in my line', is a

99

modern phrase of youth. It is sometimes used in inverted commas by older people.

SCIENTIST, meaning 'Christian Scientist'—*He's a Scientist*—is often used by members of this faith and others. It is an annoying misnomer because the attitude of Christian Scientists to life cannot possibly be called scientific.

SCORELINE; see -LINE.

SCOTCH: This is a much discussed word. It is undoubtedly correct for a U English person to say *He's Scotch*. But Scotch people of all classes say *Scottish*, except when they are referring to whisky when, like the English, they say *Scotch*. In linguistic matters *Scots* is correct—thus *Middle Scots* and *Scots* (not *Scotch*) *Gaelic*, this latter being the technical term for what is usually just called *Gaelic*—the "Scots" is necessary to distinguish this Gaelic from the Gaelics of Ireland and the Isle of Man (that is, Irish and Manx).

SCREAM: *Oh, isn't she a scream?* is a non-U expression, less used to-day than it used to be.

SCRUB as in *Better scrub it!*, meaning 'wash it out, cancel it'. This Royal Air Force term—used originally of a mission—is now considerably used outside the Service.

SCRUBBER, meaning 'promiscuous girl', is a lower-class word, which, owing perhaps to television, now has a certain wider currency.

SCURF: see DANDRUFF.

SEA: "Cheer up! Worse things happen at sea" is a cliché.

SEE: *You see* is a cliché-phrase used by many to punctuate a whole conversation. *Be seeing you!* and *See you!* are two of the many ways of saying good-bye. They are perhaps rather non-U. *Long time no see*, a cliché based upon Chinese pidgin English, may at one time have been reasonably U; now it is essentially non-U. *I'll get the dog to see him off*, i.e. to send him away, is a fairly recent expression, perhaps non-U.

SEEM: *What seems to be the matter?* is a non-U cliché.

SEE-THROUGH, as of a blouse, is a rather new word. It seems an unnecessary one, for it means exactly the same as *transparent*.

SELECT, adjective, as in *a select suburb* or *the neighbourhood is very select.* Non-U.

SELF: *a shadow of one's former self*; see SHADOW.

SELL in *to sell an idea to somebody.* This expression is much overworked. *To sell the pass*; see PASS.

SEMANTIC: This is a piece of scientific jargon, considerably used by journalists.

SEMI, meaning 'a semi-evening frock'. The thing and the word are non-U, though, to-day, many U women possess one. In big hotels the non-U change into one for dinner.

SEMINAL (of ideas). Of recent years this word has been greatly overworked.

SEND UP, meaning 'to make a joke of' and the like. This slang expression is perhaps nowadays slightly overdone.

SENIOR in *senior citizen*, sometimes abbreviated as *senior*, meaning 'an old-age pensioner or other old person'. A term deliberately introduced from America as being kinder than other expressions for the concept. In England it has but little vogue.

SERVANT: Before the last War, many servants did not much like being referred to by this word. Yet *He was a good servant* is certainly complimentary. To-day those few who have servants are still less likely to refer to them as that.

SERVICE: *Can we have some service?* is a rude thing said by the non-U when they are being kept waiting, as, for instance, in a pub, shop or garage. *It's all part of the service* is said by ingratiating shopkeepers in response to thanks. The non-U have taken it up as a facetious remark in a wider context.

SERVIETTE: Non-U, as against U *table-napkin* or *napkin*. Perhaps the most celebrated non-U indicator. Surely to-day there must be U teenagers who deliberately say *serviette* in order to annoy their parents. Paper serviettes—now almost universal—are of course non-U. U households have linen table-napkins, unhygienic because they are washed infrequently. Rich U people have clean table-napkins at every meal.

SESSION: *I had a good session with him* is a cliché. A Scotch equivalent—a *sederunt*—is however redeemed from cliché-ness by an air of Scotch intellectuality.

SET UP, verb: This originally American piece of jargon has a great vogue, particularly among those learned people who are inclined to write "bad English"—*I then set up Equation 19*. But, of course, in some cases, *set up* is correct—as in *to set up something on a calculating-machine*. The derived noun, *set-up*, as in *the whole set-up*, is jargon, and not learned jargon.

SETTEE, meaning 'a sofa-like object', is non-U.

SEW: *It's all sewed up* (or, with the alternative past participle, *it's all sewn up*), meaning 'everything is satisfactorily arranged'. Cliché-slang.

SHADOW: *He's but the shadow of his former self.* Cliché.

SHAKE: *That shook me*, sometimes *that shook me rigid*, meaning 'that upset me'. Non-U cliché.

SHAKE-OUT, noun, as in a Ministry or Department, meaning 'a reorganisation of the personnel'. Political cliché-slang.

SHAMBLES: *It's a positive shambles*, meaning 'an awful mess'. Cliché-slang.

SHAME: *It's a shame, What a shame!* is used by the non-U in a curious manner and of serious events, such as someone's death. But the phrase is used by everyone, including the

U, of more trivial matters; *it's a shame you can't come to lunch to-morrow.*

SHAPE: *I don't like kidneys in any shape or form.* Cliché.

SHARE: *Share and share alike* is a—rather old-fashioned—cliché.

SHARP, meaning 'sour', as of fruit, is non-U.

SHELL: *shell egg*; see EGG.

SHEPHERD: *Shepherd's pie*; see COTTAGE.

SHOCKER, as in *Mr. Smith's new hat is a shocker.* An expression much used by the non-U.

SHOE-HORN is the normal U word. *Shoe-lift* has a certain currency, not necessarily non-U.

SHOP: *Shop around,* denoting the trying of different places for the purchase of something. Cliché.

SHORT: *In short supply*; see SUPPLY.

SHORTFALL: A Civil Service and ministerial piece of jargon.

SHOT: *A shot in the arm* (e.g. for Industry). Cliché.

SHOULD: *Though I says it as shouldn't* is a facetious cliché—imitation dialect—used essentially to forestall a charge of boasting—*I'm very good at darts, though I says it as shouldn't.*

SHOULDER: *chip on one's shoulder*; see CHIP.

SHOW: *It's a bad show,* or just *Bad show!* This piece of Service slang has been much overworked by non-Service people.

SHOWER: *He's a shower,* meaning 'a nasty bit of work'. The original meaning of this phrase is unpleasant, but this is not realised by many who use it. It is often to be heard in films and on television.

SICK and *ill* are to some extent interchanged by the non-U. Certainly in the non-U *I was very ill on the boat,* where the U say *sick. He's sick,* for which the U say *He's ill,* may originally have been American. But the compounds of

103

sick (*sick-room*, *sick-list*), in which *sick* does mean 'ill', are normal. *Sick joke* has been overworked.

SIGNIFICANT: The statistical sense of this word ("If you toss a coin a thousand times and get six hundred heads, that is significant", i.e. the coin is biassed in favour of the head) is, oddly enough, quite correctly used by the General Public.

SILENT: *the silent majority*; see MAJORITY.

SILLY: *silly ass*; see ASS; *silly me!* see ME.

SIMILAR: This is used by bar-men to mean 'the same'— 'What will you have, sir—similar?"

SIMPLE: *It's as simple as that!*—"You can *not* park your car here; it's as simple as that". Cliché.

SIR is certainly not as much used as it was fifty years ago. But waiters still call people that, and old and/or distinguished men are often so addressed. There is a general feeling against the word, as it implies class-distinction, and many people, particularly the young, would wish to ignore this. The old, U "cross" use of *Sir—Do you realise you've run into my car, Sir!*—may still be heard, but sounds affected.

SIT: *To sit an exam* is non-U; the U equivalent would be *go in for*. *My jumper was sitting on the chair* is a female use; it is not non-U. *Sat*; see p. 11.

SKID: *To put the skids under someone*, meaning to sack them, is a cliché.

SKILL: *diabolical skill*; see DIABOLICAL.

SKINT, meaning 'broke', is a working-class word popularised by television.

SLAP: *slap down* as in *He asked a silly question and got slapped down* is cliché-slang.

SLOT as in, for instance, *the seven o'clock slot*, on television, is jargon.

SMALL: *the smallest room*; see ROOM.

SMASHING!, as in *The film was smashing!* or "*A*. We're all going to London.—*B*. Smashing!", was originally non-U, but is now used by many other people, particularly children. Some U speakers use it in inverted commas.

SMEAR, as in *a smear campaign*, is journalese.

SMELL: see ODOUR.

SMOOTH, as in *I don't like Smith; he's very smooth*, is an overdone word.

SNAP!, said for instance by someone on observing that her scarf is identical with that of the person to whom she is talking. Some consider this use harmless.

SNARE: *A snare and a delusion* is a cliché.

SNIDE, as in *a snide remark*. An overworked slang-word.

so!: Some affected people say this when they mean 'yes'— in what they think is an imitation of German. *So what!* is cliché-slang.

SO-CALLED was once employed as a term of abuse—*These so-called Germans* [but they really were Germans] in the First War. Curiously, the use continues, at least in newspapers.

SOCIETY: *affluent society*; see AFFLUENT. *In Society*; see p. 9.

SOD OFF!: A vulgar, somewhat euphemistic expression.

SOFT in *soft drink* seems to be non-U. The U person would be likely to specify what he would have and say *I'll have some tonic* rather than *I'll have a soft drink*. *Soft option*; see OPTION.

SOMETHING in *Something like that!* is a non-U tag which can be used in many contexts. "*A*. Are you going to buy some chocolate?—*B*. Something like that!", or "*A*. So you're going to tea with George and then to dinner with Cynthia? —*B*. Something like that!"

SORE: *sore thumb*; see THUMB.

SORRY: *sorry and all that*; see ALL.

SORT, noun: *It's difficult to buy a teapot of any sort or kind.* Cliché. *Sort of* is a cliché-expression used principally by children and young people—*I sort of recognised him.*

SORT, verb: *I'll soon sort it,* or even *him,* meaning 'I'll see to it/him', is non-U cliché-slang.

SOUL: *the life and soul of the party*; see LIFE.

SOUND, noun: *Sound and fury signifying nothing* is often used as a cliché, as, for instance, of the music of Liszt.

SOUND, verb, in *sound off,* as in "In a moment he'll get very angry and sound off". Cliché-slang.

SPADE: A working-class word meaning 'a black man'. To many, it is thus taboo, like *nigger* (q.v.).

SPANISH: *an old Spanish custom*; see CUSTOM.

SPASTIC: This is used by the young as in *What a spastic shot!* The use is frowned on by many, for, to-day, for some reason, spastics are more venerated than are other ill people.

SPEAK: *We spoke at 10 a.m. on Tuesday,* meaning 'we talked on the telephone'—used in letters, etc. This Last War piece of jargon seems to be little used to-day. *It speaks volumes*; see VOLUME.

SPECIAL is applied to various things in a way which some find rather nauseating—*She's a very special person,* a female use. It is supposed to be a word much used by children—and, in books, in this context, it is often written *speshul,* to make it more endearing. This is silly, because *speshul* and *special* are obviously pronounced exactly the same.

SPECTACLES: This is certainly old-fashioned U for what most people, U and non-U alike, call *glasses.* (I have even heard *my distance-spectacles.*) *Specs* is even more old-fashioned U.

106

SPELL: *spell it out*—"D'you want me to spell it out for you?'
—is a cliché.

SPEND: *spend a penny*; see PENNY.

SPIN-OFF, noun, as in *And then, of course, there's a considerable spin-off*, meaning 'further effects'. Jargon.

SPIRITUAL: *his spiritual home*; see HOME.

SPLENDID, as in "*A*. I bought that hat in Trebizond.—*B*. How splendid!" Rather overworked.

SPONGE: This is non-U for a kind of cake. The U say *spongecake*—"I made a spongecake with jam in it"—or *jam sandwich*.

SPLIT: *split the atom*; see ATOM.

SQUARE: *We're back to square one* is a cliché.

SQUIRE: This is used as a semi-facetious form of address by various people—but not much by the U. It is frequently heard in pubs—*Pint of bitter coming up, Squire!*

STAB: *Better have a stab at it*—cliché.

STAMP: *postage stamp*; see POSTAGE.

STAND: *stand up and be counted*; see COUNT.

STAND-OFFISH: On the whole this is a non-U word. It has, rather naturally, no U equivalent, because the U assume that no one will be this to them.

STARTER, meaning 'the first course of lunch or dinner', as it might be, grape-fruit. This fairly recent word is not so much non-U as jargon.

STAY, as in *Pollution has come to stay*. Cliché.

STEAM: *He was all steamed up*, meaning 'enraged' or 'excited'. Overdone word.

STEM: Stem from, as in "My dislike of apples stems from a particular incident in my childhood". An americanism, now considerably used in this country.

STEVEN: *even Steven!*; see EVEN.

STONE: *To leave no stone unturned*—perhaps the most celebrated of all clichés. Does anyone still dare use it?

STOOD: see p. 11.

STORYLINE: see -LINE.

STRAIGHT, as in "*A*. Did you take that pound note?—*B*. Straight, I didn't". Cockney.

STRAIN: *stresses and strains*; see STRESS.

STRATA: to use this as a singular is uneducated.

STREET: *It's up your street*. An overworked expression.

STRENGTH: *To go from strength to strength*. A cliché. *A tower of strength*; see TOWER.

STRESS, as in *the stresses and strains of modern life*. It is curious that this old cliché should have such a very technical origin—both terms are fundamental concepts in Elasticity.

STRING: *To pull strings*; a cliché still widely used because many persons, particularly young ones, believe that this has more effect than it actually has.

STRIP: *strip-Jack-naked*; see BEGGAR.

STUDENT: Recently this word has been used to mean, not only someone at a university, but a schoolboy or schoolgirl. It is so used in newspapers. The reason for the use probably lies with the children themselves; for some reason, they do not care to be called schoolboys and schoolgirls. This neologism is bad, because of the obvious danger of confusion.

STUDY, in *He's studying for an exam*, is non-U.

SUBJECT: *That will shed some light on the subject* is a cliché.

SUBSTANTIAL: *in substantial agreement*; see AGREEMENT.

SUCH: There is a curious use as in the following: "*A*. Have you seen any blue butterflies with white spots on their wings?—*B*. No, I haven't seen such". It is probably non-U—it is much used in the detective stories of Freeman Wills Crofts.

SUCK: *to suck someone's brains*; see BRAIN.

SUFFICIENT: This is used by the non-U in many cases in some of which the U say *enough*. "*A*. Will you have some more potatoes?—*B*. No thank you, I've got sufficient." Or, more concisely, "*A*. Will you have some more?—*B*. Quite sufficient, thank you".

SUIT, noun, applied to women's clothes is apparently now acceptable.

SUIT, verb, in *Suit yourself*—"*A*. Shall I take one of these, then?—*B*. Suit yourself!" A rude, non-U remark.

SUITE, meaning 'sofa and chairs', is non-U.

SULTRY: Used of the weather this word is non-U.

SUMMAT, meaning 'something'. This is used on television to denote a person speaking dialect. The word does actually occur in the dialects.

SUP: *To sup ale*. Exactly the same remarks apply as in the case of the immediately preceding word.

SUPER: This is essentially a children's adjective, but it is now very widely used, though often in inverted commas. *Super-duper* can also be heard.

SUPPLY: *In short supply* is a cliché.

SURE: Various americanisms, widely used in this country, may be mentioned here. *Sure!* and *Surely!* simply meaning 'yes' are of this nature, so also is the expression *That's for sure*. There is an old non-U, purely English expression, *Well, I'm sure!*, which expresses the speaker's surprise at something. No doubt it still survives.

SURPRISE in *Surprise, surprise!* is a well-known non-U cliché.

SURVIVAL: *the survival of the fittest* has become a cliché.

SWALLOW: *swallow the dictionary*; see DICTIONARY.

SWEET, meaning the after-meat course of lunch or dinner, is a well-known non-U-ism. The U still say *pudding*, but this certainly leads to silliness—can an ice really be described as *pudding*?

TA meaning 'thank you' is non-U.

TABLE: *at table*; see p. 12.

TACK: *To get down to brass tacks* is a well-known cliché, originally a facetious one, because *brass tacks* is supposed to be what someone heard *hard facts* as. There is a more modern cliché of somewhat the same meaning: *to get down to the nitty-gritty.*

TAKE: *I'll take you up on that* meaning 'One day, I'll accept your offer' has been much overdone. *Take a bath*; see BATH.

TALE: *Thereby hangs a tale.* Cliché.

TALK: There is a very annoying construction of this verb, still to be heard to-day, as in *I've been talking Chinese with him all the afternoon* meaning, not 'in Chinese', but 'about China'. *Talk of the Devil*; see DEVIL.

TANGLE, as in *I shouldn't tangle with him*, meaning 'get mixed up with'. Cliché-slang.

TART, noun; see PIE.

TART, adjective, used of fruit, etc. is non-U for U *sour*.

TA-TA meaning 'goodbye' is non-U. There used to be a non-U expression *T.T.F.N.* 'ta-ta for now'.

TATTY: A much overdone word.

TAX: *Tax evasion* and *tax avoidance* are confusing; one is legal, the other isn't. Care is therefore needed, for instance, in describing something that a solicitor may be specialising in—otherwise you may slander him.

T.B.: This is now universal; *tuberculosis* is technical and *consumption* out-of-date.

TEA: *High tea* is a meal that the U think the non-U have. But the non-U, although they do have the meal that the U think they have, do not call it this; they just call it *tea*. Hence the non-U, if they wish to refer to what the U call *tea*, have to do so by some other name; and they do, for they call that meal *afternoon tea*. So, perversely, the only people who actually use the expression *high tea* are the U; they sometimes have it, too, and refer to it by this name, as, for instance, before going to a cinema. *Cup of tea*; see CUP.

TEACHER: This is non-U for U *schoolmaster* or *schoolmistress*. Non-U children use it in the vocative (*Please, teacher!*) and as in *Teacher says . . .*

TEENY: This is a female word—*Just a teeny bit more, please*; or, *I've only got a teeny little handkerchief.*

TELEVISION: The non-U called this the *Telly*; this expression was then used in inverted commas by the U, and has finally become the natural expression of very many. With regard to the definite article it may be said that *I saw it on television* is U-er than *I saw it on the television*, but that there is no class-difference between *I saw it on telly* and *I saw it on the telly.*

TELL: *You're telling me!*, meaning 'don't preach to the converted', is a non-U cliché. *Tell!*; this was (is?) an expression meaning 'tell me about it'—as "*A.* I had a very rough time in London.—*B.* Tell!" It may well be of schoolgirl origin. *They tell me* is a cliché.

TEMPERATURE in *I've got a temperature*, i.e. fever, is, of course, really very silly, because you must have *some* temperature. It is however universal and therefore acceptable, just as much as *I'd like to sit in the sun*, which, presumably, could only be said correctly by a personified space-rocket; how silly it is is seen by translating it literally into German—*ich möchte in der sonne sitzen. To answer the door* is equally silly, since it is not the door that is answered.

TEMPLE: *The temple of health* is an old non-U expression for 'the lavatory'. Probably, it no longer exists to-day.

TENSE—*She's very tense*—is a medical jargon word, much used by the general public. Similarly, *all tensed up*.

TERM: *terms* is a landlady's or hotel word—*the terms are twenty guineas a week*.

TERRIFIC: *It's terrific!*, once a very popular phrase and one used by the U too, seems to be obsolescent.

TETHER: *To be at the end of one's tether* is a cliché.

THANK, verb: The non-U use this verb in a variety of ways. As for instance, *thanking you*, and *I thank you*, both said with a peculiar intonation which cannot be indicated in normal printing. "*A*. I'll go in the car then and you can walk.—*B*. Thank you very much!"—said sarcastically; non-U cliché.

THANKFUL: *thankful for small mercies*; see MERCY.

THANKFULLY: see HOPEFULLY.

THAT as in "*A*. She believes in Astrology.—*B*. She can't be *that* stupid!" is non-U cliché-slang.

THE: *The measles*; see p. 10.

THEM: *us and them*; see US.

THING: *I've got rather a thing about it* is overdone. *It's just one of those things* is a cliché.

THINK: *I would think* and *I would have thought* are clichés used to vary the normal *I think*.

THIS: "*This is it!*"; see IT.

THOSE: *He's one of those*, meaning 'he's a homosexual', is still to be heard, and, indeed, much overdone.

THROUGH: *From ten through two* meaning 'from ten until two'.

This americanism is much used on the wireless, but not greatly otherwise.

THROW: *throw the book*; see BOOK; *throw up*; see VOMIT.

THUMB: *It sticks out like a sore thumb*. A rather unpleasant cliché.

THUMP: *I thumped him*, meaning 'I hit him', and *I gave him a thumping*. These expressions are used on television to indicate that the user is a working-class, dialect speaker. The word is actually so used in dialect.

THUSNESS: *Why this thusness?* is a cliché.

TICKER; see DICKY.

TIGER: *paper tiger*; see PAPER.

TIGHTLY, adverb; see p. 11.

TIME: *A good time was had by all* is a cliché. *Moment of time*; see MOMENT; *from time immemorial*; see IMMEMORIAL; *long time no see*; see SEE.

TINKLE: *Give me a tinkle*, meaning 'Ring me up' (on the telephone), is non-U.

TINY: *out of your tiny mind*; see MIND.

TIP: *on the tip of one's tongue*; see TONGUE.

TISSUE: *Tissues* meaning 'paper handkerchiefs' or the like are considered non-U. But the U certainly use them too.

TITLED, in reference to a member of the peerage, is non-U.

TIZZY: *I'm all of a tizzy*. Overdone.

TOD: *On my tod*, meaning 'all alone'. This expression is, in my experience, more used on television than in real life. It is certainly non-U, if not indeed working-class.

TOFFEE-NOSED: This is used by the non-U to indicate a "stand-offish" (a non-U word) U person.

TOILET: Non-U as against U *lavatory*, or, nowadays, *loo*. Perhaps the most written about of all non-U/U distinguishing marks. The non-U have a singularly graphic use of the preposition *on* in this context: "*A.* Can I see

Mr. Smith, please.—*B*. He won't be a minute, he's just on the toilet".

TOKEN: *By the same token* is a cliché.

TONGUE: *It's just on the tip of my tongue* and *Keep a civil tongue in your head* are clichés.

TOP: *Top people* derives from an advertisement for *The Times* ("Top people read *The Times*"). It is overdone; other similar uses of *top*, meaning 'the best of its kind'—*The top croquet-players*—are harmless. *To blow one's top* is cliché-slang. So also is *It's tops* or *He's tops at darts*.

TOPCOAT: This word, once probably U, is now obsolete, and is universally replaced by *overcoat*. *Greatcoat* is in a precisely similar situation.

TOUCH as in *A touch of the Alf Smiths*, meaning something characteristic of Alf Smith. This non-U expression may still be heard, particularly on television.

TOUCH: *not to touch with a barge-pole*; see BARGE-POLE.

TOUCHÉ: It might have been thought that this expression was dead. But it was used recently by the Headmaster of Eton in a letter to *The Times* admitting that he had in fact, in an earlier letter, used an unattached participle, for which he had been reproved.

TOUGH in *to get tough with someone*. Cliché-slang.

TOWER: *She is a tower of strength* is a cliché.

TOWN meaning 'London'—*I'm going up to town*—is non-U. Certain schools use the expressions *I'm going up town* or *I'm going down town* according to the geographical position of the relevant town.

TRADE: *the rag trade*; see RAG.

TRAMP: *To go for a tramp* is affected; it is often used by nature-lovers.

TRANSPIRE is often used pompously, as in *It then transpired that . . .*

TRAUMATIC: This word is much overworked—*a traumatic effect*.

TREE: *he can't see the wood for the trees*; see WOOD.

TRICK: *He never missed a trick* meaning 'he did it all perfectly' is a cliché. *How's tricks?*, which was once (still is?) used as a form of greeting, is cliché-slang. *Very tricky* of a situation or the like is overworked.

TRIUNE meaning 'three in one' is, naturally, used of the Trinity. The peculiar use of this word by a Herefordshire parlourmaid in reference to one of those dishes that contain cheese, biscuits and butter—she called this *the triune dish*—must surely be idiosyncratic.

TROT: *On the trot* meaning first 'one after the other'—*he took three wickets on the trot*. Secondly as in *I've been on the trot all day*, i.e. going to the lavatory. Both expressions are cliché-slang.

TROUBLE: *What seems to be the trouble?* is a cliché. It is stated to be used by policemen meaning 'What's going on?' or the like. *The trouble with people like you is . . .* is a rather offensive cliché.

TRUE: As in "*A.* But the Boers were very good shots.—*B.* True!" Much overworked. *He's so bad at bowls, it just isn't true.* Cliché (non-U?). So too is *How true!*—"*A.* As I always say, children should be seen and not heard.—*B.* How true!"

TRULY in *Yours Truly* meaning 'oneself' is non-U. "*A.* Where do I get the forms from?—*B.* Apply to Yours Truly." *Well and truly*; see WELL.

TRUTH: *The moment of truth*; this is a translation of Spanish *momento de la verdad*, the moment of killing the bull in a bull-fight. It must have come into English from American, for, in general, whereas the English do not like bull-fighting, the Americans are very fond of it—they even

115

introduced it into the films of *My fair lady* and Jules Verne's *Around the world in eighty days*, in either case entirely without justification. In English, *the moment of truth*, used figuratively, is a cliché of which journalists are particularly fond.

TRY: *What you are trying to say is* . . . is an annoying cliché.

T.T.F.N.: see TA-TA.

TUMMY, TUM: Children, of all classes, are taught to say these words, and the use persists in later life. But many people—perhaps chiefly intellectuals—do not like them.

TWENTY-ONE: *free, white and twenty-one*; see FREE.

TYPE: *That type*, meaning 'that man', derogatorily—*I don't like that type, Smith* or *He's a bad type*. This translation from French—*ce type-là*—was at one time much overworked. It seems not to be used so greatly to-day.

ULCER: *He's got an ulcer* meaning 'a gastric ulcer' is un-educated, because there are many other kinds of ulcer (e.g. peptic, varicose).

ULTIMATE: *the ultimate deterrent*; see DETERRENT.

UNBERUFEN! There are still a few old U-ladies who use this German expression instead of *Touch wood!* They will have had German governesses.

UNBUTTONED, meaning 'in relaxed, jovial mood', is an affected word. It is perhaps particularly objectionable in the phrase *unbuttoned Bach*, meaning the music of Bach as exemplified, for instance, in the Peasant Cantata.

UNCERTAIN: *in no uncertain manner*; see MANNER.

UNCLE: *Bob's your uncle!*; see BOB.

UNDERPANTS: see PANTS.

UNIQUE: *Very unique* and *quite unique* are well-known to be "bad English"; indeed they could be called uneducated.

UNIVERSITY: *at university*; see p. 11.

UNSAID: *It's better left unsaid* is a cliché.

UP: *It's up to you* or *It's entirely up to you.* This cliché expression is often used rather offensively; it is a favourite of the non-U. *I'll be right up* is used by a non-U person speaking from the ground floor to a higher floor.

UP YOURS! as in "He told me I couldn't park there, so I just said to him 'Up yours!' and parked". This vulgar, probably working-class expression, is often to be heard on television.

UPSET as in *He's had a little stomach upset* or *I was upset during the night.* The use is essentially uneducated, though widespread.

UPTIGHT: This is a fairly recent americanism, to some extent replacing the earlier americanism, *het up*.

US: *He's not one of us*, a U expression meaning 'he's non-U', is not much used to-day. *Us and them*, referring to two classes of people (e.g. the haves and the have-nots) is a cliché.

USE: "*A.* Will you have some mustard?—*B.* No thanks, I don't use it." This is non-U.

UTILITY ROOM: This American word is non-U. Many people do not know what it means—*box-room* is the nearest U equivalent.

VANTAGE, VAN (as in *Vantage in!*, *Van in!*) were once non-U for Advantage in tennis. They may still persist.

VEG meaning 'vegetables' (*cut off the joint and two veg*) is non-U.

VEHICLE: To refer to one's car as *My vehicle* is non-U. The word is however natural in official use.

VIABLE: This word, from Biology, has become jargon— "The Club will hardly be viable with all those resignations".

VIS short for *visibility—vis rather poor to-day*. Harmless slang (originally Royal Air Force).

VISIT: *I must just pay a visit*, i.e. go to the lavatory, is non-U. So was *visiting card* (in its true meaning, i.e. what the U just call a *card* (= *carte-de-visite*)) and so is the euphemism *I'm afraid the dog has left his visiting card*.

VOLUME: *It speaks volumes for his good-nature.* Cliché.

VOMIT, verb: This is the usual word to-day, but many people find it unpleasant and say *be sick*. The americanism *throw up* can also be heard.

WAIT: *I can hardly wait!*, as in "*A*. I'll read you my essay on Pope.—*B*. I can hardly wait!" Overdone. *Wait on!* (as for instance in asking someone to stay at the telephone). This expression was originally dialect, but is now very generally used. The normal U phrase is *hang on!*

WALL: *Enough to drive one up the wall* is rather overdone slang.

WALLET: This is essentially a non-U word, but it is used by many who are not non-U, because they know no other.

The old-fashioned U is *pocket-book*. The status of *notecase* is not clear—also non-U?

WANT: *He wants out* (of a dog). This Scotch expression was once felt to be endearing; now it is overworked.

WARRANTY: This is used by motor-car manufacturers to mean *guarantee*. The two are in fact "the same word". In the former, Old Norman French *warantie* is preserved more or less intact; the latter receives the prosthetic *g*—normal in Old Central French (*guarantie*).

WATCH: *Watch it!* A non-U phrase used in a variety of ways: "You're always being rude to Shirley. Watch it!" (or *You want to watch it*).

WATERPROOF meaning 'macintosh'. The status of this word is not clear; possibly it is non-U.

WATERTIGHT: *He kept his business and his political life in watertight compartments.* Cliché. The word is also used as mathematics slang: *This definition is now watertight.* (When lecturing in German, the question arises whether this use may legitimately be translated *wasserdicht*.)

WATSON: *Elementary, my dear Watson*; see ELEMENTARY.

W.C.: A long established non-U-ism for U *lavatory* or *loo*. In the last War, the Germans particularly liked to refer to Churchill as this.

WEALTHY: As applied to people this is a non-U word, as against U *rich*. This is perhaps one of the best-known U/non-U distinguishing marks.

WEATHER: *good weather for ducks*; see DUCK.

WEE, meaning 'little'. Except when used by the Scotch, this is affected.

WEEP, noun, as in *She then had a little weep*, is affected.

WELCOME: *You're welcome* is a response used to someone who has said *Thank you*. Though polite, it is non-U. It is often used in shops.

WELL: *Well* is used as a punctuator by all classes. *Well anyway* can also be heard in this rôle; it is not necessarily non-U. *As well as can be expected*; see EXPECT. *Well and truly* is a cliché—"She was well and truly beaten in the Finals".

WELL-CONNECTED is a non-U word meaning 'of good family'.

WELLINGTON: *Wellingtons*; the U for this kind of boot used to be *gum-boot*. *Wellies* is used by the non-U, especially by mothers to children.

WET: *He's an awful wet* (or *he's awfully wet*), meaning that he's very dull. This harmless piece of slang is probably dying out.

WEIGHT: *take the weight off your feet*; see FOOT.

WHAT?: see EH. *So what!*; see SO.

WHATEVER: *Or whatever* is cliché-slang—"They've got everything in the deep freeze—chickens, turkeys, ham or whatever".

WHILE: see p. 12.

WHINBERRY: see BILBERRY.

WHIP: *Someone whipped it*, i.e. stole it. This lower-class expression has a certain currency outside that class; it is used on television. Cliché-slang.

WHIRLYBIRD: see CHOPPER.

WHITE: *free, white and twenty-one*; see FREE.

WHORTLEBERRY: see BILBERRY.

WICKED: *No peace for the wicked*; see PEACE.

WIN: *You can't win!* Cliché. "We succeeded in getting the Council to make up the road. Now people are complaining that cars go along it too fast. You can't win!"

-WISE, as in *Teethwise, peppermint is a bad thing to eat*, meaning 'in respect of the teeth' (it causes caries). This use of *-wise* as a suffix to a great variety of words is, it must be admitted, extremely useful.

WITH: *With it*, as in *He's not very with it*, meaning 'He's not very compos'. A fairly modern expression When used by others than the young or the non-U, it is generally said in inverted commas. *Are you with me?*, meaning 'Have you understood me?', is a non-U cliché.

WOG: see CHINK.

WOMAN: *the little woman*, meaning 'my wife', is (old-fashioned?) non-U.

WOOD: *Not to be able to see the wood for the trees*. Cliché.

WORD: *dirty word*; see DIRTY.

WORK: *all in the day's work*; see DAY. *Are you happy in your work?*; see HAPPY.

WORKING: *Working party*; see PARTY.

WORRY in *Not to worry!*, as in "*A*. I've lost that pound you gave me.—*B*. Not to worry!" Rather non-U.

WORSE: *worse things happen at sea*; see SEA.

WORST: *to be one's own worst enemy*; see ENEMY.

WRAP in *Wrap up!*, meaning 'shut up!', said for instance to a crying child. Fairly harmless.

WRONG: *Don't get me wrong* is a cliché often used instead of the more old-fashioned "Don't misunderstand me". *Put a foot wrong*; see FOOT.

WRITING PAPER: see NOTEPAPER.

YE meaning 'the', as *Ye old Englishe teashoppe*, still persists. It is essentially a misprint. The Middle English definite article was written *þe*, the first letter being the Anglo-Saxon *th*-letter (called *thorn*). In many late Middle

English manuscripts this letter was indistinguishable from Y, and thus gets so printed. *Ye* is felt to be a joke-word—*I will fetch ye chairs* can be heard among schoolboys.

YEAR: *in years*; see p. 11.

YEN: *I've got rather a yen for peaches.* This americanism has a certain currency in this country.

YOU: *I don't think that hat's quite You.* Originally female, this kind of expression is now overworked.

YOUNG: *The young*, used of adolescents, is rather affected. It is however accepted at Oxford as used of one's pupils. *Young lady*; see LADY; *young Master*; see MASTER. *We're not getting any younger* is a cliché.

YOUR: The non-U often use this in cases in which the U use the definite article—*You put your spanner on your nut.*

YOURS: *yours truly*; see TRULY.

YUGO-SLAVIAN: To say *Do you speak Yugo-slavian?* is un-educated. In English, the main language of the country is called *Serbo-Croatian* which, oddly enough, is one language not two—Serbian and Croatian are one and the same language, though, naturally, there are differences between different dialects. Serbian is however written in the Cyrillic alphabet (like Russian), Croatian in the Latin alphabet (like English).

ZERO: This is the American for the figure "nought", and the word has a certain currency in this country—*A centillion is one followed by six hundred zeroes.* Oddly enough it is not yet used in English telephone numbers—people still say *Oh.*